DISSERTATIONS

ON THE

IMPORTANCE AND BEST METHOD OF STUDYING

THE

ORIGINAL LANGUAGES OF THE BIBLE

BY JAHN AND OTHERS

TRANSLATED FROM THE ORIGINALS, AND ACCOMPANIED WITH

NOTES

BY M. STUART

ASSOCIATE PROF. OF SAC. LIT. IN THE THEOL. SEM. ANDOVER.

Second Edition.

Wipf & Stock
PUBLISHERS
Eugene, Oregon

Wipf and Stock Publishers
199 West 8th Avenue, Suite 3
Eugene, Oregon 97401

Dissertations on the Original Languages of the Bible
by Jahn and Others
By Stuart, Moses
ISBN: 1-57910-610-2
Publication date 3/12/2001
Previously published by Andover: Flagg and Gould, 1827

STUDY OF THE

ORIGINAL LANGUAGES

OF THE BIBLE.

PREFACE.

In discharging the duties of his profession, the translator of the following sheets, after perusing the several dissertations which they comprise, felt that it might be acceptable and useful, in a special manner to the young gentlemen whom he daily instructs, to communicate something from them on the best mode of conducting Hebrew studies. He began, by translating that part of Jahn's dissertation, which respects the method of study by daily and habitual repetition. When this was read to the class of which he has the special charge, by one of their number, they expressed to the translator their gratification with it, and their desire that it might be printed, in order that it might become accessible to all students in the department of oriental philology. This excited the translator to proceed in his work, and add the whole dissertation of Jahn. In order still more fully to complete a view of the best mode of conducting oriental study, he felt it to be interesting to make the other additions, comprised in parts II. and III. It may be proper here to give some account of each of these parts, that the reader may be better enabled to understand their value.

The principal author of part I. is Dr. J. Jahn,* formerly Professor in the University of Vienna of the oriental languages, biblical archaeology, higher criticism, and doctrinal theology. He is a Catholic in name, but, as will be seen by the perusal of his dissertation, a man of a truly Protestant spirit. His talents have long been known and generally acknowledged, in Germany, specially as an oriental scholar. He has published, among other works, a Hebrew lexicon; an Arabic grammar (the best except De Sacy's;) a large Arabic Chrestoma-

---

* This name is pronounced as we should pronounce *Yahn* or *Yagn*, in English.

thy with a copious lexicon; biblical archaeology in 5 vols. octavo, (the most complete work of the kind that has ever been published ;) and an excellent Introduction to the Old Testament, in 4 vols. 8vo. Besides these, he has published several editions, in German and in Latin, of a valuable Hebrew grammar. From the Latin edition of 1809, Part I. of the following sheets is extracted. It stands in the orginal, as a part of the preface, and is entitled *Disputatio*, &c. It was originally addressed to the scholars whom he taught, and printed in the first editions of his grammar, under the title of *Oratio*, &c. It may not be improper to add, that Jahn* is considered in Germany as one of the most enlightened and staunch defenders of the divine authority of the sacred books, and the inspiration of their authors; and generally as inclined altogether to defend those views of religion, which are commonly denominated orthodox.

Under Part I. is also comprised the view, which the celebrated J. D. Michaelis, Professor at Göttingen, and author of a multitude of works in almost every department of philological, historical, and doctrinal literature, has taken of the best method of studying the languages. It is extracted by Jahn, from a recent publication which contained it, and is made a part of his dissertation. It is retained here, in the same connexion in which it appears in Jahn's Hebrew grammar; as the separation of it from Jahn's work would occasion an undesirable chasm in it.

Part II. is translated from the preface to the small Hebrew grammar of Gesenius, (3d edition, 1818,) who is probably the best Hebrew scholar in Europe. He is the author of the best dissertation on the Samaritan Pentateuch; of the best Hebrew lexicon and grammar; and of the best critical history of the Hebrew language, which have yet appeared. It was thought that the views of such a scholar, on the subject of Hebrew study, would be very acceptable and useful to students and instructers.

Part III. contains an extract from the dissertation of the celebrated Wyttenbach, Professor of Greek at Leyden, printed in the preface to his *Ἐκλογαι Ἱστορικαι*, or *Selections from the Greek Hisrians*. This dissertation has been recently translated and published by the Hon. J. Pickering of Salem,† who, amidst the numerous calls

---

* Since the above was written, sacred literature has been called to mourn over the loss which it has sustained, by the death of this distiguished man.

† Now of Boston.

of public, professional, and private duties, still finds or makes time to cultivate letters, and specially Greek philology; a knowledge of which he has acquired to such a degree, as may serve to administer reproof to the great mass of men liberally educated, who make the futile excuse for abandoning the study of the classics, that *they have no time to pursue it ;* and one might truly add, to reprove many a teacher too, whose sole or principal business it is to cultivate a knowledge of the Greek. So true is it, that a lover of literature, a genuine son of the Muses, will always contrive to gratify his taste. *Amor vincit omnia.*

The principal object of printing here the extract from Wyttenbach, is, to give force to the recommendations of Jahn, that the student should repeat perpetually the preceding lessons, until he becomes perfectly familiar with them. Such advice from two consummate masters in different departments of philology, cannot but make some impression on those, who consider the nature of the human mind, or the importance of such experience as Jahn and Wyttenbach had acquired.

It is to be hoped, that the substance of what is here inculcated may be taken into serious consideration, by all our teachers in schools and colleges. It is high time that the subject of practical education should receive more attention in our country. If the following sheets should, in any measure, contribute to excite the attention of our literary public to this great work, the translator will be richly rewarded for his labours.

Of the notes which are added, but little need to be said. They are miscellaneous, and are *designedly* so. It was hoped that they might prove the more attractive to young minds, on this account; and for such, they are principally designed. Some explanations and modifications of the sentiments in the dissertation of Jahn were proper. It may be said, that the notes are too diffuse. But it was much more difficult to compress them within their present limits, than it would have been to make them more copious. From many others, which might easily be added, the translator thought it his duty to refrain, lest he should make a book and not a pamphlet.

In regard to the method in which he has translated the dissertation of Jahn from the Latin, and those of Michaelis and Gesenius from the German; he has only to say, that it has been his object to translate freely, and give the sentiment rather than the mere form of the expression. The construction of the original sentences is very seldom retained. Indeed to do this would be impossible, without obliging every reader to turn away with displeasure.

The German mode of forming sentences is so involved and composite, that no English reader of any taste could endure it in an English dress. The translator has sometimes made four, five, or more sentences out of a single one in the original ; and of course has been obliged to add the necessary particles of connexion and transition. After all, he fears that some of his readers, at least, will find foreign idioms in his translation ; as the publication of it followed the execution of the work so soon, that there was not time to cool from it, and come to the correction of it as one would to the work of another person.

That the whole may prove acceptable and useful, specially to our rising youth, the hope of the church, is the sincere desire of the

                                    TRANSLATOR.

PART I.

JAHN'S DISSERTATION.

—••◉••—

J EROME in his letter to Sophronius says, "a Jew, when dis-
puting with you, and wishing to elude the arguments which you
adduce, will affirm, as often as you quote any passage of the Old
Testament, *It is not so, in Hebrew.*" Such an opponent may
every theologian now have ; and if he is unacquainted with the
original languages of the Bible, he must either have some Jerome
at hand whom he may consult, or he will be thrown into great
perplexity, since he professes to teach what he has not himself
learned. A dexterous opponent in theology, (and opponents
there are, in our age, both numerous and respectable for talents,)
may not only answer, like the Jew, for the sake of eluding your
arguments from Scripture, but in serious earnest may reply, much
oftener than is commonly supposed, that the Original does not
convey the sentiment which you assign to the Translation.* In
such a case, the weapons which the theologian had borrowed from
his version of the Bible become useless ; nor can he find, in all
his store of erudition, any thing by which he can defend himself
against the attacks of his adversary. Nor is he able *satisfactori-
ly* to convince himself. It will avail nothing to urge the authority of the interpreter, on whose version he expected to rely ; for
let the interpreter be Jerome himself, or any one more learned,
and diligent, and lucid, and even more holy, still he is ignorant of
many things which might be learned. Nor can a translator always
remember what he does know, so as to recall it at the moment

---

* See note A.

2

when he wishes to recall it.   Besides, he does not *always* bestow
that degree of attention upon his work, which is requisite ; and
consequently he will sometimes render the words of the sacred
writer in a manner which is ambiguous, incongruous, or unseem-
ly.   As he is but a man, so he is liable to err ; and of course he
will *sometimes* miss the sense of his author, and translate him in
a faulty manner.   Of this, any one unskilled in the original is not
able to judge ; and consequently no theologian, who is thus unskilled, can determine whether any translation be true or false.

I should be unwilling, indeed, to affirm with Isidore Clarus,
that there are not less than eighty thousand errors in our Vulgate translation.   But, on the other hand, I would not willingly
undertake to plead the cause of the Vulgate, against so able a
writer.   I shall, however, very readily concede that many things,
and even most things, are rightly translated in all versions of the
Bible ;* and in the better ones, that the errors are few, and not
very important.   Yet this does not weaken the force of what I
have said : for no version is without faults, and consequently it
must remain an established position, that no theologian, unacquainted with the original, can ever be certain respecting the
translation of any passage ; because he cannot separate those
things which are rightly translated from those which are wrongly
translated ; nor see any reason why the one is correct, and the
other faulty.   Of course he must grope in darkness.

Even a selection of the better versions cannot be made, without much and refined knowledge of the originals.   He must depend, therefore, on the judgment of others to select for him.   I
will not say that this is unworthy of a theologian ; but certainly it
is very *insufficient* for him ; for so often as the better versions differ from each other, (which happens not unfrequently,) he must
be at a loss which to prefer.

Perhaps some one may imagine, that he can compare a number of versions together, and thus elicit the true sense of the
original.   Origen, in ancient times, endeavoured to facilitate
such a method of studying the Scriptures, by his Hexapla.†   His

---

* See note B.   † See note C.

work is thus described by Jerome ; " Origen has compiled a copy of four versions, written out and arranged opposite to each other, so that where one disagreed with the original, it might be corrected by the agreement of the others."* But the insufficiency of such a comparison was readily perceived by the celebrated Montfaucon ; who says, "This method of attaining to the true knowledge of the original meaning is very uncertain, and by no means free from danger ; for it often happens that the majority of versions are erroneous, and one only is correct."†

In very many places, in which there is no dissent among the versions, one who is ignorant of the original language cannot *fully* perceive the meaning of the sacred authors. No version ever can adequately express, in all cases, the meaning of the original. All who have any acquaintance with the business of translating, will readily acknowledge this. Words in different languages, which have a *general* correspondence to each other, very often do not correspond in *all* respects ; sometimes signifying more, and sometimes less. In the *phrases* also which are appropriate to each language, there is the same or a still greater difference. Hence the interpreter must often be at a loss to know by what word or phrase he shall, in the most adequate manner, express the sense of the original. Not unfrequently, he must content himself with having found in his own language a word or phrase, which, although it does not fully convey the sense of his original, approximates as nearly to it as may be.

The difficulty now stated is still greater, and recurs oftener, the more diverse the genius is of the languages of the original and the translation. This remark applies, in its full extent, to the original languages of the Bible. The Hebrew and the Chaldee of the Old Testament, were the languages of an oriental region very diverse from ours ; and the Greek of the New Testament, in respect to the ideas which are attached to words, in regard to phrases, and to the whole tenor of language, is conformed to the oriental tongues. The languages then of both the Old Testament and the New, differ as much from the western tongues, as the oriental fashions of dress differ from ours.

---

* Pref. in Paralipom.   † Praelim. in Hexap. Tom. I. p. 9.

Besides, our sacred books were written many ages ago; since which, many significations of words have been changed in various ways, and circumscribed sometimes within wider and sometimes within narrower limits. The consequence is, that oftentimes it is extremely difficult to find in our languages any words, by which those ancient words can be in any tolerable manner expressed. If therefore, as we have seen, even the better versions cannot, in all respects, adequately express the original, but necessarily express sometimes more, and sometimes less than the sacred writer does; it is evident that the theologian, whose duty it is to investigate every thing with nicety, and accurately to define and describe the limits of every sentiment, can in no way fully discharge the duties of his office by merely consulting versions.

We may come to the same conclusion, by arguing from the *nature* of versions. These may be divided into those which are literal, and those which follow the sense of the original. If the interpretation be merely *literal*, all the phrases which are peculiar and appropriate to the oriental languages, (and many of these are very important in theology,) remain so obscure, that they still need an interpreter to explain them. If the peculiarities of idiom be neglected, and phrases of this kind be adapted to any vernacular language, then a sense is often put upon them which is foreign to the meaning of the original. Nor can a commentary upon the original be read or understood, without a knowledge of the language on which it is written; it cannot therefore be adapted to produce conviction as to the meaning of the original.

If the translator, without striving to be *literal*, merely aims at giving the sense, this will often embarrass the reader who is unacquainted with the original language. He will not be able to understand how the original can convey a meaning, so different from that which he has obtained through the medium of literal versions. But should he trust to his interpreter, he cannot ascertain what reasons he has for so doing; nor defend the versions which he credits; nor give a reason in favour of it, to others who impugn it.

I would now ask, whether it may not very properly be demanded of a theologian, as a man of learning, that he should neither affirm nor deny any thing in theology, without being able to assign some good reason for it? In such a predicament, what could a theologian effect, in an age like ours? Every day, novel interpretations of most important passages are produced, which not only glitter with the splendour of a specious philosophy, (of which indeed the sacred writers knew nothing,) but are confirmed, as is pretended, by arguments drawn from the genius of the oriental tongues; so that it requires a thorough knowledge of these tongues, and great attention and diligence, to render any one able to judge in these matters of what is true and what is false. How shall one, who has no acquaintance with the originals, be able to judge? And yet it is necessary to form a judgment. One cannot suspend his opinion and withhold his judgment, so as to remain neutral; for many novel interpretations are of such a nature as to shake the very foundations of revealed religion.

The considerations which have now been stated are of great importance, and ought to excite our young men, who devote themselves to theology, to diligent and animated exertions in order to acquire a knowledge of the original languages of the Bible. Nor are other arguments wanting, which, though less weighty than those already produced, are by no means unimportant.

There are many passages of Scripture still, that labour under some critical or hermeneutical difficulty; and which nevertheless have, or at least are supposed to have, an important bearing upon some points in theology. Difficulties which belong to either of these classes cannot be touched in a translation. Hence the theologian, who relies simply upon his interpreter, being ignorant of any difficulty in the original, uses a translation with confidence, and builds his argument upon it, and thus exposes himself to be despised, or sneered at, by an opponent who understands the original.

Difficulties of a critical nature, scarcely any of the ancient interpreters, and but few of the modern ones, have touched upon.* Now as there are a variety of readings in many passages, and only one of these can be expressed in any translation, which of course must be the reading that the translator prefers; and as his judgment cannot be supposed, by any one who is acquainted with these matters, always to be correct; how shall he who is unskilled in them, be able to satisfy himself whether the right reading has been preferred? Where a reading is doubtful, a theologian should satisfy himself as to what is genuine, before he can use the passage as a proof text, or can reject it as dubious, or not pertinent to his object. But to do this, a knowledge of the original language is necessary; for one who is destitute of this, can not judge of the words of the original; nor if he reads a critical commentary can he understand it.

In respect to difficulties of a *hermeneutical* nature, more or less of them are unavoidable. A translator, we will say, has given the sense of his author, according to his best judgment. The question still remains, Is it the *real* meaning of the author? This question involves inquiries respecting the meaning of words and phrases, or the principles of syntax, in the original language; which if one does not understand, he cannot understand the real state of the question, much less can he decide upon it.

Now since there are many passages, which are attended with either critical or hermeneutical difficulties, and yet these difficulties cannot at all appear in a version, persons who can use merely a translation are exposed to use it without caution, and to build with much effort very important doctrines upon it, while they are unable to see, that with all their labour they are accomplishing nothing. To exhibit the truth of this by apposite examples were very easy, did not the limits of this dissertation forbid it.

I cannot forbear suggesting here, (what is fundamentally connected with the science of theology,) that if the *genuineness* of the sacred books be rendered doubtful, their authority is weakened, and the whole edifice of theology is overturned. Yet this *genuineness* cannot be established, without a refined and intimate knowledge of the original languages of Scripture; for it depends,

---

* See Note D.

in a great measure, upon the genius of language and style, which differ among various authors, and in different ages. Every age and author has something peculiar as to phraseology, or ornament; or some other marks which have respect to the style, or the general conformation of language, or the colouring of it. If now the language and style are repugnant to the genius of the author, or the age in which the book purports to be written, then the work is regarded as spurious, and as belonging to some other author or age, whose language and style it resembles. The art of criticism judges not only concerning whole books, but parts and particular passages of books; so that any part, or passage, the language and style of which does not accord with that of the writer or the age to which the book is assigned, is reckoned among interpolations. Notable controversies have arisen, during the present age, as to the genuineness of whole books, and many parts of books. The arguments used in these controversies, are principally drawn from the nature of the style and language; and these arguments cannot, therefore, be understood or judged of by any person ignorant of the original language of the books. Can he then be called a theologian with propriety, who has not learning enough to judge of the arguments, by which the genuineness of the sacred books is attacked or defended?

Two points are fundamental, in the science of revealed theolgy: the one, that the sacred books are of supreme authority, (which cannot be shown if they are not genuine); the other, that the true sense of them should be elicited and established. But who can support the genuineness of them, or elicit their true sense, without a refined and intimate acquaintance with their originals? And can it be compatible with the duty of a theologian, to be doubting on these subjects, and not to be established on an immoveable basis?

Those then who affirm that a theologian does not need a knowledge of the languages, overturn theology itself, at least a refined and fundamental knowledge of it; so that it is difficult to speak in an adequate manner of their temerity, or to determine what they design or wish. If any one, therefore, desires to impugn what I have said, the *truth* will easily defend it, although I remain silent.

I could wish that those students in theology, who promise
to themselves an adequate knowledge of this science without studying the languages of the Bible, and those divines
who impugn the necessity of this study, and either by express
words, or by a sneer, endeavour to dissuade young men from
pursuing this mode of study, and retard the progress of those
whom they cannot dissuade, would weigh these things and ma-
turely consider them. If these opponents will not imitate Cato,
(who, excited by the love of philosophy, learned the Greek language in his old age,) at least let them learn silently to permit
that others should pursue these studies. Very different from
these men was Augustine the famous bishop of Hippo, who, although ignorant of Hebrew (as he confesses), and but a tyro in
Greek, yet very plainly tells the truth, when he says; " The
men whom we have undertaken to teach, besides the Latin language, have need of *two other tongues*, viz. the Hebrew and the
Greek." A little after, he repeats the same sentiment; "Because of the diversity of translations, the knowledge of those languages is *necessary*."[*]

In the same year, this celebrated father wrote thus to Jerome,
the most skilful linguist of that age; " So important does your
knowledge appear to me, that if possible I should pursue my
studies by clinging to your side. But as I cannot do this, I
think of sending to you some one of our children in the Lord,
whom we are bound to instruct, if you will give me leave to do
it." From this, it is evident how great the estimation of this most
learned bishop was of the knowledge of languages; and how
great his reverence for an interpreter of the Bible, who was furnished with this knowledge.

In regard to Jerome himself, it is unnecessary to say any
thing; for it is well known how much time he devoted to the
study of languages, and how much envy and calumny he drew
upon himself thereby; to all which, in his epistles, he sometimes
replies facetiously; sometimes, gravely; and not unfrequently,
with asperity.

---

[*] Lib. II. De doctrina Christ. c. 9.

Many other fathers of the church, as Chrysostom, Basil, and Theodoret, although ignorant of the languages, yet recur constantly in their writings to the interpretation of words made by Origen and Jerome; and by this appeal, they have demonstrated the importance of the study of the languages, in a stronger manner than they could have done by words. From a proper view of the importance of this study, we may easily account for it, that in every age, those theologians have been most distinguished, who had a profound knowledge of the original languages of the Scriptures.*

But enough has been said on this topic. It now remains to show, that in our age it is not sufficient for the accomplished theologian to possess a knowledge of Greek and Hebrew only. The kindred dialects of the Hebrew, specially the Aramean and the Arabic are important; and without a knowledge of these, it is in vain to expect a refined and accurate knowledge of the Hebrew itself. The arguments by which this is supported, are now to be distinctly considered.

The holy Bible, as all agree, is the principal souroe of theology; the fountain from which, in a special manner, all science of religion is drawn; the foundation on which its doctrines are built. But to build the superstructure in a secure and lasting manner, it is necessary that the sacred books should be *rightly understood;* in other words, that the same meaning should be attached to all the words and phrases, which was attached to them by the sacred authors themselves, and their cotemporaries; or that the same sense should be given to words and phrases, which the common usage of that age, country, and nation gave to them. Every thing here depends on the *usus loquendi;* so that whatever is not either directly or indirectly deduced from it, is necessarily uncertain and unstable.

This *usus loquendi,* however, is a simple *historical fact.* To discover what it was, we must investigate what meaning the ancient Hebrews attributed to the words and phrases of their vernacular tongue; and this, like other historical facts, must be es-

---

* See note E.

3

tablished by proper testimony. This fact none could know with
certainty, except the ancient Hebrews themselves; and they
only are witnesses fully competent. But the testimony of these
we have not, except what the sacred books themselves contain;
and these are too few and too brief to exhibit all the words and
phrases, in such a connexion as admits of but one meaning, and
thus limits the sense so as to allow no room for doubt. And besides this, many a controversy arises, as to what words really belong to a variety of passages in holy writ.

The Greek of the New Testament, moreover, is not such as is
found in ancient Greek authors; nor can it be learned from the
study of these alone. It is a dialect, which the Jews (and consequently the writers of the New Testament) spoke and wrote, in
the primitive ages of Christianity. It is intermixed with many
Hebraisms, Chaldaisms, and Syriasms; and many of these may
be illustrated by the use of the Arabic language. The understanding and illustration of the New Testament, therefore, depends very much on the knowledge of the Hebrew, and its kindred dialects.*

We must consider also that the Hebrew, for more than twen-
ty-three centuries, has been a dead language, (as the Greek and
Latin have for a long time been,) and that but few remains of
it are extant. It is not, like the Greek and Latin, still exhibited
in a multitude of books, but in the few comprised in the sacred
volume. Nor have we any version, lexicon, or commentary at
hand, which is cotemporary with it as a spoken language, and a
witness of the *usus loquendi* that is fully competent. The most
ancient versions are several centuries younger than the Hebrew,
as a vernacular tongue; and consequently the authors of them
could have no personal acquaintance with the *usus loquendi*. The
testimony to which they could get access, was not wholly free
from exception, as they themselves clearly evince, inasmuch as
they sometimes differ from each other, in the translation of passages, and thus by implication impeach each other of ignorance,
or at least render each other's knowledge suspected. Not unfrequently too, they translate in such a manner as to make no sense
at all, and thus impeach themselves.

---

* See note F.

The Jewish teachers have, it is true, preserved some knowledge of the Hebrew tongue. But the writings derived from them are much more recent than the versions just mentioned. Besides, they often disagree among themselves ; they attach a meaning to many words and phrases, which is manifestly erroneous. Not unfrequently they assign to words a meaning which is deduced from their philosophical tenets ; sometimes they sport with serious things by eking out mystical meanings from the letters ; and finally, they every where show that they stand upon uncertain ground, in regard to the knowledge of the ancient *usus loquendi* of the Hebrews. In a word, the Jewish Rabbins bear such a relation to the ancient Hebrews, as the Scholastics of the middle age do to the ancient Latins. As the latter are not competent witnesses in respect to the ancient *usus loquendi* of the Latins, so neither are the Rabbins as to that of the ancient Hebrews, from whom they are very remote. Yet still, the Rabbins and all the Scholastics have preserved no inconsiderable part of their ancient language. All the commentaries, scholia, and lexicons are much more recent than the older Rabbins and versions. They are partly drawn from these sources ; partly built upon erroneous hypotheses ; compiled without accurate criticism and knowledge of the Hebrew ; and at variance among themselves ; which must always excite distrust. The most recent commentaries are preferable ; but these cannot be fully understood, without a knowledge of the cognate dialects ; nor do they always agree with each other ; so that some tribunal to which we may appeal, in order to settle their contesting claims, seems to be necessary.

We have now seen, that there is no *direct* testimony to which we can appeal, respecting the *usus loquendi* of the ancient Hebrews. We must then supply this defect, as far as possible, by *indirect* testimony, i. e. by the cognate dialects. These exhibit, in a multitude of cases, the same words as the Hebrew, the same phrases, the same grammatical structure and conformation of language, and therefore belong *essentially* to the same language. They differ only in smaller things, which is occasioned by the diversity of dialect. The *usus loquendi* of the Hebrew, Chaldee,

Syriac, and Arabic, (provincialisms excepted,) is the same ; and
hence the *usus loquendi* of either cognate dialect, is a competent
witness in respect to that of the Hebrew.   In Syriac and Arabic,
there are a multitude of books, from which *idiom* may be learned ; nor are lexicons and commentaries wanting in these languages, (specially commentaries upon the Arabic poets,) the
authors of which spoke and wrote these languages.   Nay, the
Arabic is still a living language, and is now spoken from the
straits of Gibraltar to the Ganges ; and *substantially* the same
language as the ancient Arabic, is still used in Arabia.   Here
then is a living testimony to the point in question, widely diffused through the world ; so that the fact after which we are inquir-
ing, spontaneously presents itself.   Hence a knowledge of the
Hebrew may be rendered in a good degree certain; and the
more so, the more deeply we penetrate into the genius of the
kindred dialects, specially of the Syriac and Arabic.   No other
dead language can, like the Hebrew, boast of living sisters, who
may testify in respect to its idiom and meaning.   And these witnesses not only testify in regard to the meaning of words and
phrases, but exhibit tropes, allegories, images, and figures of
speech, peculiar to the oriental tongues, and of a bold commanding nature, partly the same which the Bible exhibits, and partly
similar to those which it contains.*

What has now been said may be sufficient to show, that no
one who is truly worthy of the name of a theologian, can be ignorant of the original languages, in which the Bible was written.†
There is no need that I should add to what has already been
produced, by referring to examples of erroneous and distorted
interpretation of the Scriptures, the offspring of ignorance in respect to the original language.   It were easy to multiply examples of this nature, on all sides.   But those, who are just com-
mencing these studies, and for whom I write, would not be able

* See note G.

† It will be very evident to any one, that I am not speaking at all, in this
dissertation, respecting catechists, or instructers of a secondary class ; but
only of an *accomplished theologian.*   Let catechists, without any knowledge
of Greek and Hebrew, be multiplied to any extent which you may desire ;
but let not such call themselves theologians.   [AUTHOR'S NOTE.]

to understand them ; and to recite them would carry me much beyond the limits assigned to this disquisition.

It remains now, that I consider the objections alleged against this view of the subject which I have exhibited ; examine the complaints which are made, in regard to the difficulty of studying the oriental languages ; and finally say something respecting the best method of teaching and learning these tongues. Let us first hear the allegations which are made against the study of the languages.

1. Our opponents attribute peculiar efficacy to the following argument ; viz. " *Our ancestors were distinguished theologians and excellent preachers, without any knowledge of Greek and Hebrew.*"

Far be it from me in any measure to detract from that reverence which is due to our ancestors, or tarnish the lustre of their characters. What I contend for, may be made evident to all ; and it is simply this. The state of theology is *now* very different from what it *formerly* was. What was unnecessary in other times, has now become indispensable to the theologian. All literary studies, at present, and specially that of philosophy, (with which theology is closely connected,) have advanced much beyond their former state ; not only comprising much more than formerly, but being treated in a much more subtile manner. Theology therefore neither can remain, nor ought to remain in its former state, unless you would, in a criminal manner, expose religion to danger ; which follows, of course, when theology is neglected. Theological literature, with all other learning, has recently taken a much wider range than in former times ; it comprehends vastly more now, than it once did ; and must be pursued with greater diligence and exertion. Let the young men then, who are well instructed in philosophy, and accustomed to nice and subtile disquisition, pursue a similar course in theology, and learn to investigate every thing in an accurate manner. Unless they do so, what they hear and read, during their theological course, will profit them but very little ; nor will they be able to profit others.

In a special manner, the meaning of Scripture is to be investigated by the solid principles of interpretation ; to be defended against the attack of others; and in places of greater importance to theology, to be so established, that the proper doctrine may be deduced from it, in a manner not to be fairly controverted. This we have already seen cannot be done, without a knowledge of the original.

The study of the languages, therefore, which our ancestors, who were not accustomed to nice discrimination in theologizing, might supersede, cannot be neglected by us; unless theologians are to be formed, who are not qualified to satisfy their own minds, much less to meet the exigencies of the times. The inquiry should not be, What kind of theologians our ancestors were ; but rather, What kind of theologians do the present age and state of things demand ? An age in which literature, in all its branches, has made peculiar progress, and which requires corresponding advances in theology. If the improvements, which have been made in philosophy, medicine, and jurisprudence, even in the art of war too, are not despised or neglected, although our ancestors were ignorant of them ; neither should we despise or neglect improvements in theological knowledge, although our ancestors were unacquainted with them. Any one guilty of such neglect, not only proclaims his sloth, but his general indifference in respect to theological study, and religious doctrine.*

Should any one complain, that the study of the languages is too *laborious*, I may send him to the very heathen for advice; one of whom thus writes, "Youth should, in a special manner, be disciplined by labour and patience both of mind and body."†

2. A second objection is, "*that very few ever become distinguished philologists and interpreters.*"

But did the objector never observe, that very few ever become distinguished philosophers, naturalists, mathematicians, historians, physicians, lawyers, doctrinal theologians, and preachers ?

---

* See Note H.   † Cicero, De Officiis, Lib. I.

And yet, who ever questioned the utility of these sciences? Why is the study of language only exposed to this objection? Is there any consistency in such a complaint? Nor is the objection more weighty, when it is alleged,

3ly. *" That almost every person, who studies the languages in the schools, and expends much time and labour upon them, afterwards forgets what he has learned, and is unable to pursue his studies for want of books."*

Does not the same thing happen, I would ask, in regard to all the sciences? And as in these, so in respect to the languages; it is the fault of the learners, who having overcome the first difficulties of the pursuit, flag in their course, and choose rather to lose by negligence what they have acquired, than by further effort to convert it to use, and to reap the benefit of it. A youth may be indulged, perhaps, in passing more lightly over many studies which are required, and by which he may receive a kind of polish, and be prepared for important stations in life; but not so, in the study of languages. The theologian always needs these, to understand the original sources of religion. *" The want of books"* is a mere pretext to conceal sloth and indifference. This is evident from the case of multitudes, who are in no want of means to purchase books, and yet neglect study. On the other hand, those who are earnestly engaged in this pursuit, by some means or other always obtain the necessary books.*

Perhaps too, as it respects the patronage of such studies, the words of Cicero may, not unaptly, be applied to this subject; "The less that honour is conferred upon the poets, the less the study of poetry will flourish. If any persons of distinguished genius in this way have arisen among us, they have not, like the Grecian bards, been crowned with glory. Can we suppose, that if Fabius, a nobleman of the most distinguished rank, had been eulogized for being a good painter, there would not have been a host like Polycletes and Parrhasius, in our country? Honour nourishes the arts; and all are urged forward in their course of study, by the prospect of distinguished reputation.

* See note J.

On the contrary, those arts which are held in contempt, always continue to be neglected."*   But,

4ly, " *These foreign commodities,*" say others, " *cannot be offered to a Christian people. The study of languages, therefore, cannot contribute at all to the instruction of the multitude. Much more judicious would it be, if young men, without the apparatus of languages, would learn to expound the Scripture in a plain way, and with such a knowledge of the Bible go into the sacred office of the ministry.*"

If every thing, which does not immediately belong to the instruction of Christians at large, is to be banished from the schools of theology, then must the study of philosophy, of ecclesiastical history, of canonical law, of systematic theology, and of the learned part of moral discipline, as it is now pursued in the schools, be excluded. The whole apparatus of erudition is, indeed, but little adapted to the multitude; still, a theologian should be conversant with it, in order to qualify himself either clearly to understand the doctrines of religion, and separate them from erroneous opinions, or to teach them to the people in a lucid manner, so as to produce the effect of persuading them. And here the preacher needs a knowledge of the original language, as often as he appeals to the testimony of the Scriptures, which should be rightly understood and explained. Not that he should make use of philological disquisition in his public discourses; but that the true sense, which by the assistance of philology he has obtained, may be stated in a perspicuous way, without any mention of the original words. If I may so express it, not the shell of erudition, but the nut of doctrine is to be given them; and a clergyman ought to be a learned man, that he may break the shell, and come at the nut.†   But if the teacher knows only a little more than the people whom he instructs, to say the least, his discourses must be very jejune and unimportant.

Jerome, in former times, was much addicted to complaining of teachers who were ignorant of the Scriptures. In his epistle to Paulinus, he thus writes; " What belongs to medicine,

---

* Tusc. Quest. Lib. I.   † See note K.

physicians teach; artificers instruct in the knowledge of the arts; the art of explaining the Scriptures is the only thing, which every body understands. *Scribimus indocti doctique poemata passim.* The garrulous old woman, the prating old man, the wordy sophist—all—engage in this business. They mangle the Scriptures, and teach before they have learned. Some with their eye-brows knit together spout forth great swelling words, and philosophize among old women about sacred literature. Others, O shame! learn of women what they are to teach to men; and as if this were but a small matter, they descant with audacious flippancy, in public, upon things which they do not understand. ——I say nothing of those who hold the same office as myself, and who after the acquisition of a little secular knowledge, come to the Scriptures, and in a set discourse sooth the ears of the populace. Whatever they utter they think is the law of God; nor do they deign to inquire what the prophets or apostles thought, but heap together incongruous testimony to make out the meaning which they give; as if it were some great affair, and not a most vicious method of teaching, to pervert the meaning of the Scripture, and to make it speak as they wish, contrary to its true sense. What! have we not read Homeric centos, and Virgilian centos? Virgil then, though he never heard of Christ, must be called a Christian, because he wrote

Jam redit et virgo, redeunt Saturnia regna ;
Jam nova progenies coelo demittitur alto.

It is the Father too addressing the Son, when Virgil says,

Nate, meae vires, mea magna potentia solus!

And the Saviour too is described as speaking on the cross, when the same poet says,

Talia perstabat memorans, fixusque manebat.

These things are mere puerilities, and worthy only of mountebanks. To TEACH what you are ignorant of! Nay, (for I cannot but speak with indignation,) not to have knowledge enough, to know that you are ignorant!"

This epistle of Jerome is attached to our Vulgate version; and although it was, in former times, so often copied by the

monks and others, and is now printed in all the editions of
the Vulgate, yet the vehement invective of this holy father
proved to be insufficient to rouse ecclesiastics from their slum-
ber, and excite them to the study of the Bible.   In fact, they
did neither read the Bible itself, nor this epistle of Jerome ; or
if they did read it, they deigned not to consider its contents.
Hence, even in our age, it has been necessary for the civil law
again and again to admonish them, and strongly to urge them,
lest the study of the Bible and the languages should be neglected.   Whether this be decorous for the clergy, let those consider, who think that young theologians may undertake to explain
the Scriptures without the aid of languages, and that these are
unworthy of their attention.   But such qualifications of the clergy do not meet the calls of the present day ; nor do they satisfy
the young men themselves, who being accustomed to the study
of philosophy, and to ask a reason for every thing, of their own
accord ask a reason for any particular translation or exegesis.
This, indeed, they would be compelled to do by their opponents,
in respect to many passages which are of the highest moment
in theology.   But of this, I have already said sufficient in the
previous part of this dissertation.

   That young men should go into the clerical office, with a
good understanding of the Scriptures, is both our wish and that of
our opponents.   This can certainly be accomplished in a much
better manner, if the original Scriptures are well understood and
explained ; and if we discharge our duty in this respect, our audi-
tors will not be wanting in the performance of their part.   The
reason why our opponents prefer that method of instruction,
which is so incompetent, to this which is so much more excellent, is not one which promises any thing to the dignity of the
ministerial office, or to the good of the church.

   But 5ly.   Others, who perceive the trifling nature of the objections hitherto discussed, captiously inquire, " *What advantage
now does the study of languages promise ?   Disputes enough, to
be sure, are springing from it ; but as to any good—we are not
able to discover it.*"

It is easy to perceive, that men who reason thus are unacquainted with the state of theology, in the past and present age;
for all who understand this subject, know how very different things
at present are, and how great advances have been made in religious learning. But to these inquirers I would beg leave to pro-
pose another question, viz, Of what advantage has the science
of logic been, in past times? And if they reply, (as they must,)
that every thing which has been accomplished in philosophy
has been accomplished by the art of logic, and could not have
been effected without it; then I would gently hint, that they
may apply the answer which they have given, to the study of
the languages.

It is unnecessary here to enumerate all the benefits which
flow from the study of the languages; for to dispute with men of
this class, is not only disagreeable and troublesome, but for the most
part useless. They persevere in adhering to the assertions which
they have once made, and will not listen to any arguments. They
are quite at ease, so long as there is any theology, and a Christian
religion, and a ministry; and are entirely unconcerned about
what character these may sustain. They busy themselves about
little local matters, and do not at all consider what the Christian
church at large demands; and for many things of the greatest
importance, they pompously exhibit their contempt.

In regard, however, to the controversies which are said to
arise from the study of the languages; the objector should call
to mind, that controversies existed before the study of the languages flourished. Let him look into the obsolete scholastic
theology of former days, and he will see that the different schools
of theologians were heated to an excessive and reprehensible
degree, by the warmth of disputation. Controversies are not
wanting, in other sciences besides that of theology. These are
not placed to the account of the sciences, but attributed to the
variety that exits among learned men, in respect to erudition, talents, knowledge, and temper. Nor are they regarded as being
so great an evil, that all the schools and libraries are to be locked up, so that they may speedily come to an end. Why then
are controversies charged solely upon the study of the languages?

Besides ; if any still think that the study of the languages only is to be condemned, let them beware how they oppose the
constant and unanimous opinion of the whole church ; who, although she has approved of versions, has always provided that
these should be published under the inspection of learned linguists, and carefully corrected by comparison with the original.
She has adopted the Vulgate thus corrected ; and in so doing,
has declared that a knowledge of the languages is necessary.

It will not be inapposite, if I subjoin here what Cicero formerly said concerning controversies.   " So far," said he, " are we
from wishing to have no one write against us, that we court it as
a privilege.   In Greece, philosophy had never been crowned with
so much honour, had it not been made to flourish by the disputes
of the learned.—Wherefore, I have always been pleased with
the custom of the Peripatetics, and of the Academy, who discussed both sides of every question that arose; for otherwise, you
cannot determine what is most probable respecting any topic."*
And again ; " This is the old Socratic way, to reason in opposition to the opinion of others; for in this way Socrates thought it
was probable, that the truth would be elicited."**

But granting that theological controversy is an evil, still that
it is not so great an one as some imagine, those will easily believe who are accustomed to inquire whence controversies
arise, and whither they lead.   Gold tried by the fire continues
to be gold ; nay, being separated from the dross it becomes still
purer.   One might even say with Aulus Gellius, *Truth is the
daughter of time ;†* but I choose rather to say with the apostle
Paul, " Other foundation can no man lay, than that is laid, which
is Jesus Christ.   Now if any one build on this foundation, gold,
silver, precious stones, wood, hay, stubble ; every one's work
shall be made manifest : for the day shall reveal it ; and it shall
be manifested by fire, for the fire shall prove every man's work,
what it is.   If any one's work which he has executed shall abide
[the trial], he shall receive a reward.   If any one's work shall

* Tusc. Quaest. Lib. II.   ** Ibid. Lib. I.
† Noct. Att. Lib. XII.

be burned up, he shall suffer loss; though he himself may be
saved, yet as by fire," 1 Cor. iii. 11—15.*

But it is time to quit this subject, and proceed to consider the
difficulties, with which, as many complain, the study of the oriental languages is encompassed.

But in the first place, we have a prejudice to combat, which
may easily deter men of fine talents from studying the languages ;
or persuade them, under the pretext of *difficulty*, that they may
not only neglect them without disgrace, but even add something
to their reputation by such neglect.   It is an opinion pretty pre-
valent, that men of extraordinary genius are rarely endowed with
an uncommon memory.   Hence the languages, which depend so
much on the memory, cannot be learned by them without very
great effort.   Besides, success in this pursuit would evince that
the memory is good, and so diminish from the reputation of genius or of sound judgment.   In many cases both of these considerations united operate successfully, so as to prevent all serious
effort at philological improvement.

This opinion, however, is extremely erroneous.   Those who
decry the faculty of memory, plainly show how little reason they
have to boast, on account of *sound* judgment.   For in order to
exercise a sound judgment, and nicely to discriminate between
things, a man must readily call to mind all the *criteria* by which
their differences are known, and all the circumstances in which
they are placed.   How can this be done, without the exercise
of a sound and ready memory?   On the other hand; he who has
a weak and treacherous memory, which easily forgets these criteria and circumstances, must of course be exposed to judge very
preposterously.   Superior judgment, then without a good mem-
ry, is a thing impossible.   And hence it is very plain, that a feeble memory is no evidence of a sound judgment.

Our opponents appeal to the example of old men, whose faculty of judgment often remains in full vigour, while the memory
is very much impaired.   Nicer discrimination, however, would
lead them to see, that the memory of old men is feeble only in

* See note L.

respect to recent occurrences. Their judgment respecting past
occurrences is very sound; but here the memory is sound too,
and seldom fails faithfully and readily to suggest whatever they
desire. But neither their judgment nor memory is very sound,
in regard to what is recent. For the most part they condemn
whatever has been recently discovered or instituted, however excellent it may be; and easily forget whatever they may learn in
their old age.

Thus much, however, the truth requires us to concede; viz.
that there are *some* men, remarkable for strength of memory, who
have very little sound judgment; because they want that ready
intuition of mind, by which they might survey and compare every thing which the memory suggests.

On the other hand; general experience, as attested by history, shows that distinguished emperors, kings, and learned men,
whose achievements and productions have been the subject of
admiration, were endowed with uncommon strength of memory.
What history relates concerning the memory of Cyrus, Artax-
erxes Mnemon, Themistocles, Mithridates, Scipio, and Hadri-
an Cæsar, is well known. Cicero testifies that Lucullus, in the
Mithridatic war, exceeded the expectations of all; he celebrates
him as a superior commander of an army, and assigns as a reason for it, "that he had a kind of divine memory."* One may
daily observe men of excellent judgment, who also have a very
retentive memory. On the other hand; many of a feeble memory are deficient in judgment. There are others still, whose
memory and judgment are unlike; the memory being strong,
but the judgment weak. But of these I have already spoken
above.

Experience in accordance with reason testifies how erroneous it is, to maintain that men of strong judgment possess weak
memories, and learn the languages with difficulty. Experience
also teaches, that even men of more feeble capacities may acquire a good knowledge of them, provided their studies are directed in a prudent and suitable manner. We draw this infe-

* Acad. Quaest. Lib. IV.

rence from the fact, that no person is of so feeble capacity, so dull and stupid, as not to learn his vernacular language, even in early childhood ; and that with very little difficulty. And yet a child has to make out the meaning of all *abstract* terms, (as this does not depend on the perception of sensible objects,) from adjuncts, and from the connexion of words with which he is already acquainted ; a process sufficiently laborious, but one to which adults are not subjected.

In those places where two languages are spoken, most children, at a very early period, learn them both with the same facility. A boy, eight, ten, or twelve years old, residing for a year or two in a foreign country, easily learns its vernacular tongue. In fact, a child from the age of two to six years, will learn at least four vernacular languages without any difficulty, and as a matter of amusement, if he be educated by men who speak these different languages, and speak no other while they are with him.

Hence it is manifest, that to learn languages is not a difficult task in itself ; it is made so, only by the method in which they are studied. Adults are unwilling to imitate children, in their mode of learning them. They refuse to proceed along with a moderate gait, and to go as it were on foot, and leisurely ; but are desirous to pass over hills and mountains at a single leap. They are unwilling to ply their task with assiduity, and unweariedly. They do not hear and read with sufficient attention, *nor repeat as often as is necessary.* They do not give that liberty to the memory which is indispensable, but force it, in order to learn things by rote. They do not accustom themselves, as children do, to associate with every word the thing which it designates. In fine, in a great variety of respects, they adopt a method of study, which serves rather to hinder than to help them. And in respect to teachers, let them well consider what Cicero has said, " That there is an art of teaching, as well as an art of knowing."*

Let us now examine the difficulties which occur in the

---

* De Leg. Lib. II.

study of the oriental languages, and investigate the causes of
them ; so that we may learn how to remove, or at least to diminish them.   Experience teaches us, that there are three difficulties attending this subject.   Two of these are of a grammatical nature ; one of which arises from the great difference between the oriental characters or letters and ours ; the other,
from the inflections of words that are to be impressed upon
the memory ; which however is not very formidable, as the inflections in the oriental languages are far less numerous than in
the occidental ones.   A third difficulty exists in the languages
themselves, in which there are so many words that nearly resemble each other ; so many meanings of words, designated in
various ways ; so many phrases altogether different from any in
the occidental tongues; all of which must be impressed on the
memory of the learner.

A greater difficulty than any of these arises, no doubt, from
the violence which learners are accustomed to do to the faculty
of memory, when they earnestly strive to learn every thing by
rote, or at least to retain it in their memory.   By efforts of this
nature which are overstrained, they fatigue the memory, de-
prive it of its natural vigour, and debilitate it ; whence it comes,
that they remember what they obtain in this manner with the
greatest difficulty, and of course easily forget it.   The memory
loves freedom, and is refreshed, nourished, and strengthened by
it.   In a state of freedom, it easily treasures up any thing ; but
when violence is done to it, it is burdened and weakened, so
that what is obtruded upon it easily escapes.   Daily experience
affords satisfactory proof of this. 'When we charge the memory
with something to be done on the morrow, it often happens that
we forget it ; but if, without striving to impress the memory,
we request some one to remind us of what is to be done, the ad-
monition for the most part becomes unnecessary, for we easily
recollect it.   So it often happens, moreover, that we labour hard
to recall something to memory, and the more we labour, the more
unable are we to recollect it; but when we abstain from the effort, after a short interval, the memory being restored to its liberty, of its own accord recalls what we desire.   On the other

hand, we often strive to forget something which is disagreeable ; but all in vain, for it perpetually harasses the memory even when this faculty is feeble. One might almost say, (as Themistocles did to a person who boasted that he could teach the art of remembering,) "I had rather learn the art of forgetting ; for I remember what I do not wish to remember, and cannot forget what I wish to forget."

Since it is clear then, that the memory grows strong by the enjoyment of freedom, but is oppressed and weakened by violence, it cannot be denied, that if those who study languages strenuously labour to commit *every thing* to memory, they will render their progress much more difficult than it will be, if they pursue a course which leaves the memory more at liberty.

The memory therefore must be left free, that it may retain its natural force and vigour, so as to receive impressions voluntarily, deeply engrave them, and easily preserve them. Such is the case with little children, who *spontaneously* learn any language, and often do it by way of amusement. Languages should be learned by efforts that are free, and often repeated, rather than by violent efforts. This is a point which cannot be too strongly urged. Little children, for example, whose minds are unembarrassed and free from any violence, by *constantly* hearing others speak, soon attempt to express their own ideas in a similar way. In like manner, adults who learn languages from books, with a similar freedom of mind, SHOULD DAILY READ, REPEAT AGAIN AND AGAIN THE READING, HEAR OTHERS READ, WRITE OUT WHAT THEY READ, AND PERUSE AND REPERUSE IT, AND ASSIDUOUSLY PERSEVERE IN THIS EXERCISE OF REPEATING, until what is read be deeply engraven upon the memory.

When I speak, however, of *assiduously persevering* in this exercise, I do not wish to be understood as urging to continue it for whole days, or even many hours, without intermission ; for this would fatigue, and weaken, and oppress the memory, and impede the progress of the student, rather than accelerate it. Care should be taken, therefore, not to urge the work without interruption, beyond a proper length of time. I should advise any one, not to apply himself more than one or two hours, with-

5

out remission ; and then, after attending to other business, or exercise, to return again to his task.

For example ; a part of an author, which has already been studied, and is understood, should be attentively read three or four times over, without any intermission ; then, after attending to other occupations, or after an interval of one night, let the same passage be read as many times more ; and this not merely *mentally*, BUT READ ALOUD, SO AS TO BE DISTINCTLY AND AUDIBLY PRONOUNCED. It is almost incredible, how much the *reading aloud*, so often repeated, will assist the learner. The reason of it is evident, viz. that the mind is affected not only by the letters which the eye sees, but by the sounds which enter the ear ; and thus, from the united agency of both causes, it receives stronger impressions than it could from the agency of only one, and therefore more easily retains what is impressed upon it.

It will be highly useful, also, if the learner accustoms himself to connect with the words which he reads, not merely the words by which he translated them, but the *thing itself*, that is designated by the original author. The effect of reading in this manner, when often repeated, will soon manifest itself, and demonstrate the truth of the maxim, *Legendum potius* MULTUM *quam* MULTA ; and *Gutta cavat lapidem, non vi, sed saepe cadendo ;* i. e. reading frequently repeated is better than to read a great deal ; and, drops of water wear away stones, not by violence, but by continual repetition.

How great the power of frequent repetition is, may be illustrated from the case of unlettered men, who, although of rude, uncultivated, and obtuse mental powers, not unfrequently repeat the prayers which they hear daily, after a short time, although they have paid but little attention to them, and made no effort to commit them to memory. I have known rustics repeat the Lord's prayer in Latin, which they have often heard recited in the church, though they never designed to learn it by rote. In a word ; as frequent repetition is the soul of all studies, so it is, in a special manner, of the study of languages. By this, not only language itself, but grammar also is to be learned. Nothing more is requisite to accomplish this, than that the paradigms of the inflections should be frequently read, and other words declined agreeably to them. *Let this exercise of inflection, more-over, be* WRITTEN DOWN. Why should the student reluctate at this, when it will soon become a mere amusement to him? Uni-versal experience teaches, that the writing down of paradigms, and parts of speech which are well understood, contributes very much to the learning of the dead languages. And the reason of this is plain; for in the act of writing, we delay a longer time upon every letter which we make, than when we merely read. Hence the impression upon the mind is more powerful; for the longer any cause operates, the more powerful is the effect.

The difficulties to which I have adverted above, are greatly diminished by the repetition of reading and writing, as now re-commended. Indeed, those difficulties which arise from the multitude of words, significations, and phrases, that are to be treasured up in the mind, will scarcely be felt. Seneca long ago recognized this truth, when he said, Whatever is the subject of often repeated thought, can never be eradicated from the memory; which loses nothing, except that which has not been frequently considered.

Patience indeed is necessary, in exercises of this nature. One should not be out of humour, or in a rage, if a word, or an idea that occurs, should chance to slip from the memory, so as to render a new investigation necessary, by recourse to the lexicon. If this process be submitted to with patience, the word or the idea will ultimately cleave to the memory more firmly, than if it be thrust upon it in a fit of indignation. If the course above recommended be pursued for some years, the stu-dent will perceive, that he can learn the languages without any effort which differs much from that which children make, in learn-ing their own vernacular language. It is true, indeed, that children have some advantages which adults cannot enjoy; such as freedom from cares and business, and a memory at leisure and therefore the more tenacious. On the other hand; there are difficulties in the way of children, from which adults are freed. Children are destitute of the ideas, which words are designed to convey; specially of abstract ideas, and notions of intellectual and invisible objects, which are to be gathered from the tenor of a discourse, but which are explained to adults by teachers, or by a lexicon. In many other respects too, adults possess better advantages; as their minds are matured, their faculties cultivated, they have many ideas already, and the analogy of language is explained by grammar. If therefore children can learn three or four different languages at a time, without trouble, and as an amusement, why should adults complain of learning the Hebrew, and its cognate dialects which so nearly resemble it? *Is it not a shame for adults to shudder at a task, which children can perform by way of amusement?*

In learning the grammar of any language, what occasions the most trouble is, the multitude of things which resemble each other and follow on in close connexion. Similitude occasions confusion; and where similitude exists between a great many words, the memory is apt to retain them only in a confused manner; although it easily retains a great number of things, if they are definitely distinguished; or in case they are similar, provided they occur or are presented successively, at intervals, and after what had gone before is well understood. An example will explain my meaning. If a military commander should call by name, and make to pass in review before me, 28 soldiers in uniform both as to dress and arms, I should scarcely remember the name of a single individual so as to repeat it, in case I met him afterwards. In like manner, if the 28 forms of the Hebrew letters, or the equal number of verbal inflections are presented continuously, scarcely any one will be remembered. But suppose the military commander summons five or six of the soldiers daily to appear before me, and gives me time to consider the different form and stature of each individual; tells me how this one and that received the wounds which occasioned his scars; what one and another achieved in such or such a battle, or in the assault of such a city; what is the disposition, virtues, and vices of each individual; and then shows me the spoils which each one has borne away in triumph from the enemy; and finally adds something respecting the arrangement of the army in each battle or assault; all these things I shall remember, because they are so unlike each other, and entirely distinct. The consequence will be, that I shall easily distinguish between the 28 soldiers who are brought before me as above described, learn to call them by name, and retain in my memory the different facts which are descriptive of each. So, if a similar method be pursued in regard to Hebrew letters, vowel-points, diacritical signs, and inflections of words, all these may be impressed upon the memory without any difficulty. Therefore, in going through with the grammar, a great number of things of the same kind, or very similar to each other, should never be continuously presented, much less without explaining wherein the difference consists between them and the things which have preceded. When similars are presented, the individual characteristics of each should be noted, and then things dissimilar and of another kind should be subjoined. In the arrangement of a grammar, systematic order must be pursued, so as to render it convenient for consultation ; but teachers and learners should by no means be confined to this order, unless they mean to create much useless trouble for the memory.

It may be well to illustrate this principle by an example. During the first lecture on the Hebrew, after premising some things respecting the origin and number of the alphabetic characters, let five or six of them be drawn successively, choosing those which are the most simple, and are made up of only one or two strokes. In respect to each letter, let the lines or strokes then be the subject of remark, i. e. describe them as right, oblique, perpendicular, curved, or horizontal ; and so the angles, either as right or obtuse. At the same time, the derivation of these lines and angles should be described, or what the original shape of the letter was intended by the inventor to represent ; whence it will be very evident, what changes its figure has undergone. To these five or six consonants let four or five vowels be then annexed, and at the same time, the manner in which they are read in conjunction with the consonants be explained. Next, you may draw several entire words made up of these vowels and consonants; first, monosyllables ; then dissyllables; and the mode of reading these should be explained. Some things may then be subjoined about nouns and verbs ;

such however as may be understood without a knowledge of the letters.

The learner must then commit these to memory, in private, by repeating and writing them in the manner which has been above described ; and this should be effectually done, before the recurrence of the next lecture.   In this lecture, the same method should be pursued in further explanations ; and so in the following lectures, intermixing with each something about the letters, vowels, diacritical signs, pronouns, nouns, verbs, and finally, particles.   As soon as the acquaintance of the student with the vowels and consonants is sufficient to read some of the personal pronouns, some one of them should be given him as an exercise, to be written out ; and at the same time, the inflection of a verb in the corresponding person should be given him, that he may see how its inflection is connected with the pronoun ; and all these are to be written over in private, and impressed upon the memory.

The letters and vowels being finished, (which may easily be done in four or five lectures,) in the next lecture, let something of translating be introduced, which will necessarily require the exercise of reading, and at the same time furnish words, with the meaning of them, and also the inflection.   For translating, some easy passages should be selected, which at the same time are important and entertaining.   On those niceties of grammar, which are beyond the reach of a beginner, you should not dwell, but give him to understand that those things will occur again, by and by, when they will be very plain to him.

The reading of Hebrew is generally a difficult thing for a beginner.   At first then, let him read but a small portion, which should be explained.   As reading becomes more familiar, the exercise of translating may be increased, and grammatical analysis be gradually introduced.

It is advisable for learners, not only to note particular words with their signification, but (at any rate during the first stages of study) to write out at length each part or fragment of any word, that has been explained.   This will help their memory, and their reading and writing, very much.   Let them take care not to represent the oriental letters by those of their own alphabet; for this may be a great hindrance to them, without profiting them but very little.

In this way learners, in a few weeks, will have made some sensible progress; in particular, if they are faithful in REPEATING the lectures, as I have above described : and from this progress, they will gather fresh courage. As you proceed, the exercise of translating may be increased, and that of grammatical analysis diminished, and in the space of five or six weeks discontinued. *The whole grammar is not to be exhausted at once;* for in this way, the labour becomes tedious and troublesome to a learner, and in a great measure useless ; for learners cannot remember dry grammatical precepts, until they have occasion to make use of them, by the recurrence of examples. *At first then those parts of the grammar are to be selected, which are specially important; in particular, the paradigms of inflections, omitting the exceptions and anomalies.* These and many other things comprised in a grammar are to be read and studied in private, and committed as occasion may require, or leisure permit ; and then, whenever it is necessary, they are to be adduced in order to illustrate or confirm interpretation. In this way, as they will occur in the midst of other things which have no similitude to them, and in examples where the interpretation requires the use of them, they will very easily be remembered. By constant exercises of this nature, above all if the proper repetition of them be kept up, (a thing which can never be too much recommended,) the study of the languages will be relieved from difficulty, and rendered practicable and easy.

Another observation of great importance to our subject, and which can be applied in a variety of ways, is, that the stronger any impression is made, the more tenaciously it cleaves to the memory ; and the more pleasant and agreeable it is, the stronger will the impression be. Hence it follows, in the first place, that it will be of great use, in the acquisition of the oriental tongues, if they are agreeable to us, and we feel interested in them. Books therefore should be selected for study, which treat of things that are worthy of being studied and known, and contain knowledge which is not common ; or which allure by their argument, or delight by their eloquent diction. No translation of these should be read previously to studying the books; lest curiosity be abated, either in regard to the matter or the style.

Besides these, there are other things which may assist in rendering the impression made by reading more strong and agreeable ; or, on the other hand, remove those hindrances by which the impression is weakened, and rendered ineffectual. It may be useful to suggest them in regular order.

I. Whoever has seriously turned his thoughts to this subject, cannot but have observed, how incommodious it is to translate from one dead language into another; e. g. from Hebrew or Greek into Latin. This arises not merely from the fact, that Latin is not so well understood, or not so familiar to us, as our vernacular language ; but from the circumstance, that it is as it were a foreigner, and so less grateful and agreeable to us. Besides, after making a Latin version, we again translate *mentally*, into our vernacular tongue ; and it is only after this is done, that the idea of the object designated by the word comes fully before the mind. In this way the whole train of ideas must undergo a double process, in order to be presented to us; which is superfluous, and soon becomes disagreeble, and consequently contributes to weaken the memory.

Here I would remind the student of what I have said above ; viz. that the *object* which any word designates should always be thought of, whenever the word occurs. I may add here, that the reason why the acquisition of language is so easy to little children, is, that in part the things designated by the words which they learn, are objects of the senses ; partly, that they make out the sense of words from the connexion of the discourse, exercising their power of conjecture or invention; which probably augments the impression. Now he who teaches the dead languages cannot adopt this practice too often ; I mean that of exhibiting the object, or of stopping where it is necessary in order to describe it. I know it is with some difficulty that those who have been accustomed to translate into Latin should immediately connect the idea of an object with the name of it ; for

they have been accustomed to come at this idea, only in a cir-
cuitous way through the medium of two languages. Yet I must
recommend the method of translating immediately into the vernacular tongue, so as to acquire the habit of carrying the mind
directly to the *object*, when the word which designates it occurs.
The series of ideas becomes shorter, in this way ; the impression
therefore is more forcible, being increased by the circumstance,
that our vernacular language is more familiar and agreeable to
us.

I know, indeed, that translating into Latin was prescribed to
the schools, a few years since. But this was not done for the
sake of promoting the study of languages ; for who does not
see that it must operate as a hindrance ? The object of the law
was of quite a different nature, to describe which does not belong
to our present design. So much I may be allowed to say, that
until this law is repealed, what has been inculcated above may at
least have respect to private studies, in which learners may translate every thing into their vernacular tongue. They will not find
these precepts useless ; but after a little time perceive their utility, by the progress which they make in understanding the genius
and idiom of the language that is studied.

II. In translating, no more need be said, than what is necessary to explain the word or phrase in question. Things which
are of course implied by the translation, need not be perpetually
repeated. For example, if one translates אָמַר, *he said*, it is sufficient ; he need not always add, it is a verb of the third person,
singular number, masculine gender, praeterite tense, &c ; all this
is implied by the translation. The constant repetition of such
dry things, and a copious description of all the grammatical forms
which are plain from the mere version itself, is of no advantage
to the student, but rather serves to create disgust; at least, it
crowds the memory with empty things, and does violence to it ;
not to speak of the loss of time which it occasions, nor to say
how much it detracts from the opportunity of explaining the proper interpretation or real meaning of passages.

A man of great eminence, and, as all agree, a very superior
scholar and excellent teacher in the languages, very properly

advised students, whenever they heard the lecture room perpetually resounding with nothing but grammatical forms, to forsake it, because they might depend upon it, that with great trouble and labour, they would really learn but very little, by such a method of study.

III. In teaching the languages, wherever opportunity offers, (and this will perpetually occur to a scholar of real learning,) useful and entertaining remarks are to be interspersed, drawn either from the languages themselves, or from other branches of literature, with which oriental learning has an extensive connexion. The mind is greatly refreshed by unlooked for entertainment of this kind; and it connects the ideas thus suggested, with the words which gave occasion to them, and so the memory easily preserves both. Grammatical observations of this nature I have interspersed through my Hebrew grammar; e. g. concerning the primitive shape of the letters and their successive mutations; concerning the primaeval forms of the pronouns; the inflection of verbs by the addition of personal pronouns, &c. In translating, the knowledge which every good scholar must have, will supply him with a fund of useful and pleasant observations. In this exercise, the primaeval notion attached to words may often be marked, and the successive derivation of secondary ideas from it be traced; or the origin of phrases differing specially from our own idiom may be explained. Observations of this nature, however, should neither be too frequent, nor too minute and diffuse; they should be brief and comprehensive, so as not to detract from the proper time allowed for interpretation.

IV. *Reading* and *interpretation*, in all study of languages, is the *great object* in view; and to this, every thing else must be subordinate. Study should be so conducted, then, that not only passages which are read should be frequently reperused, but that a great deal should be read and explained. Both of these objects are perfectly consistent with each other. In public lectures, much ground may be travelled over, and carefully described; in private studies, all these things may be repeated again and again. All languages are learned by use; and the use of the dead languages must be acquired in the way of repetition and frequent reading. All real progress in the dead languages most certainly depends on the exercise of interpreting them. Wherefore, as I have said above, we should not delay for a long time upon the study of grammar alone ; but after getting possession of the general and fundamental principles and forms, leave the exceptions, syntax, &c, to come in as occasion may call, and proceed directly to the exercise of translating, which will constantly afford occasion for reference to all the unstudied parts of the grammar. If any one should commit a whole grammar to memory, and neither read nor interpret the language, he cannot be acquainted with it. But he who reads and interprets a great deal, learns grammar of course ; just as little children obtain a practical knowledge of grammar by learning their vernacular tongue. Grammar is merely the medium of learning languages with more facility ; but the medium is not to be so commuted for the ultimate end, that more pains should be bestowed on the former than on the latter. I am not ignorant, indeed, that a knowledge of every part of grammar is necessary for any one thoroughly to understand a language. All which I mean to deny, (and this I would strenuously deny,) is, that a knowledge of the whole is necessary for the tyro. If such an one understands the rudiments of grammar, at the outset, by practice he will come to a knowledge of the rest. A *complete* knowledge of grammar must spring from an extensive acquaintance with the language itself. It follows, therefore, that in teaching and learning the languages, the great thing to be aimed at is the constant and ready interpretation of them. When progress in this is uninterrupted, addition is continually made to the stock of words whose meaning is known, and which occur in various forms and with different significations, and in different constructions. In this way, they are not only engraved more deeply upon the memory, but the analogy and idiom of the language is better understood.

V. In this way of teaching, or in a way resembling this, (for I by no means suppose that what I have said makes a rule, to which nothing can be added, and from which nothing can be subtracted,) learners can be carried forward, so that in a few months they will begin to exercise their own strength, and both translate and explain, before it is interpreted for them. And in this exercise, they should use a lexicon, that they may learn the difficulty of accurately translating the original, and accustom themselves to overcome this difficulty, by a careful comparison with the context. After this, one or more of the students, at a lecture, may be put upon interpreting some passage which has not been explained, and assisted occasionally, as he may need, by his instructor. Such exercises, as they compel the student to attend both to the meaning and connexion of words, are very useful to him; they disclose to the teacher also what progress the student has made, in what he is defective, and consequently what points need to be insisted on in future lectures, and what may be passed over by touching them lightly. In this way too, learners will find the grammatical difficulties that may occur, the solution of which, they are to seek from their grammar, their lexicon, or their teacher; and thus they may acquire a thorough knowledge of the grammar.

Whatever is explained, or by whomsoever, let the translation of it be made, in private at least, in the vernacular tongue. Let this be done not in a careless manner, but with great diligence. And to secure this, let the translation of some student be read at public lecture, and amended by the teacher, whenever it is necessary. Diligence in this way, as I know by experience, will achieve incomparably more than all the technical and disagreeable labour to commit grammatical rules and exceptions to memory, which, while interpretation is neglected, can never be thoroughly understood by the student.

What I have said thus far, is designed rather for learners than teachers, who generally, at present, make use of a somewhat similar method. It seemed proper to admonish learners, that they ought not to be discouraged, when they hear of the oriental languages being taught by rule; a thing which, from their ignorance of the subject, they might suppose to be preposterous. I shall easily persuade them, I am inclined to think, that the method here recommended, or one like to it, is the only one which reason and experience approves. No doubt there will be some, who will adhere to the old grammatical way, established, as they aver, by the experience of ages ; and who will accuse me of innovation. After all my experience on this subject, I might perhaps disregard the trifling objections which some adduce, who never studied languages with critical nicety. But lest learners should be moved by these objections, I will reply in a few words, as to the point respecting *innovation*, which is alleged against the method in question.

So far is it from being new, that so long ago as A. D. 1766, J. D. Michaelis inculcated the same sentiments, in substance ; and they have been generally approved by all intelligent men, down to the present period. In proof of this, I extract a passage from the book entitled *Universal Grammar*, edited at Leipzick in 1807, by J. D. Hensel. In the Preface, pp. 23—29, may be found the following passage.

"I know of but one method of teaching language, either publicly or privately, which will stand the test, and to which I am partial, not out of prejudice, but on account of a conviction of its advantages, which is derived from experience. One should first teach the student to decline the regular inflections of the language, and leave the anomalous parts with only casual references to them. After practising a little in the reading of the language, he should immediately commence the translation of it into his vernacular tongue, first in an *oral* manner, and then in *writing*. To help the memory, after he has written out the translation, let him write the original under it, or in a separate book. This practice, at least in respect to the more difficult passages, should be continued for some time, until the learner has acquired considerable dexterity in translating ; and so, by degrees he will impress upon the memory, words, phrases, and constructions.

One should not teach grammar all at once, or perpetually,

but partly by occasional remarks, and partly by previous instruction. The *precepts* either of general or particular grammar, should be taught as opportunity occurs. So also the *principles*, as well as the application of them, must be inculcated ; and at the same time, in connexion with this, some grammatical analyses should be made, but without perpetually dwelling upon them, according to the ancient mode ; for this becomes repulsive to the student. Besides, these analyses are spontaneously presented to the student, who from the first has been accustomed to decline, conjugate, and compare. The scholar who translates correctly, must, in his own mind, go through with a grammatical analysis. Lectures wholly devoted to general or particular grammar, can be given with profit, only after the student has attained considerable skill and ability in translating. In the first stages of study, such lectures would be dry, and often useless ; being too philosophical and abstract for beginners. If retained at all it will be by mere force of memory, and not because they are understood. After the scholar is accustomed to reason and criticise, such lectures may be profitable ; as the examples then adduced for illustration may be understood and compared. It is only in such circumstances, that these lectures can be intelligible ; and of course, they belong only to more advanced scholars.

I must not be considered here as inculcating a method of teaching altogether novel and untried. I have experience in its favour ; and I warn others against departing from this way. It is a great loss of time, first to teach how to decline and conjugate with entire facility and correctness ; then to treat of all the anomalous forms of the language, and to urge on the study of these, before beginning to translate. Such a method only delays, quenches the spirit of the student, and takes away all pleasure and satisfaction. This incessant grammatical hammering is not adapted to students.

To learn a foreign language, the first object should be to seize that which can most easily be impressed upon the memory. What one principally needs then, in the first stages of study, is to be presented with such words and sentences as are well adapted to this purpose.

In this way the student attains, almost without knowing how, and with much ease, to a knowledge of any tongue, which it would cost excessive and unnecessary trouble to acquire in the other method.

One question still remains. Shall the student read so as to advance with some degree of celerity, or delay for a long time on every passage? I answer; Both methods are to be connected. The mode of everlasting criticism, investigation, observation, and correction, is not at all adapted to *beginners*. Such are desirous of knowing the contents of the piece, which they are studying. Nor does even the more advanced scholar wish to be always acting the critic; he sometimes wishes to enjoy his author. In lecturing, therefore, one should pass on, with some degree of rapidity; but still not without some remarks on the matter and the language. Only the more weighty remarks, however, should be made. Leave the others, until another opportunity; which cannot fail to occur. One should endeavour, if possible, to keep the student attentive to his business, through the whole lecture, so that no remark, or word may escape him. Only very difficult works, which one goes through with advanced scholars, and to which the attention is only occasional, should be read critically and dwelt upon, and all the grammatical remarks made, which the text may suggest. The anxiety of teachers to let nothing remain unsaid which can be said, makes them much too diffuse. It renders the student indifferent too; for in this way perpetual repetition must occur."

Thus far Michaelis. I may add, that unless I had so long ago as 1792, and again in 1799, published the sentiments of the preceding dissertation, I might seem to every person skilled in teaching the languages to have extracted them from Michaelis; so similar are his views to those which I have inculcated.

It is unnecessary to add any thing to excite young men to the study of the languages, which has been shown to be so important to an accurate and solid knowledge of theology. I shall leave this to teachers, who will not be wanting, I hope, both by word and example, to excite the minds of their pupils to undertake and accomplish these studies. The importance of the subject, and their own love of this kind of literature, will urge them to do this.

I must not omit one consideration, before I close. There are many things in the Bible, which still need illustration from oriental literature. The field is very wide, and the cultivation of it highly useful. Much fruit may be reaped, to the advantage of the church. The Scriptures may be better interpreted, and thus become more useful and efficacious. To conclude; solid and lasting reputation will be acquired by those who engage in these studies with exalted views, and pursue them with unremitting ardour and diligence.

PART II.

EXTRACT FROM GESENIUS.

----●◖●◗●----

To gratify a number of instructers who take a lively interest in promoting the study of the Hebrew, I shall subjoin a few remarks on the method of teaching it, which are specially intended for the schools; although I am aware, that to persons of reflection who are acquainted with the subject, these remarks will contain little or nothing that is new. What I am about to suggest, is the result of experience; and is in brief as follows.

After the first exercises of learning to read *mechanically* are past, (and these are best accomplished by means of catalogues of words, orderly arranged, with the meaning placed by the side of them, so that the student can understand what he reads,) let the learner next be put upon reading the personal pronouns, because these lie at the foundation of all inflections in the verb. These should be impressed upon the memory, and then he may proceed immediately to the paradigm of the regular verb, which should be repeatedly read, and *orally* explained; in particular, the *characteristics* of the ground-forms (the third person of the praeter, and the infinitive or imperative) in each conjugation should be dwelt upon, and the meaning of praeformatives and afformatives be pointed out. After these explanations, the *regular verb, part by part, should be committed to memory, in the most accurate manner;* because so many other grammatical inflections are built upon it.

Before you proceed to the irregular verbs, it will be proper to give some instruction respecting the suffix-pronouns, both as connected with verbs and nouns. The student must also acquire a definite knowledge of the quiescents, and their various muta-

7

tions ; as the greatest part of the changes in the irregular verbs depends upon these.

In order to dispense, as much as possible, with all mere mechanical committing to memory, the teacher should go over each new paradigm with his pupils, and explain it *orally;* pointing out the departures from the structure of the regular verb, and the characteristics of its forms. In this way the memory will be very much aided, and the power of observing the analogy and structure of the language will be called into action, and very much strengthened. When the learner sees how מָצְבָה and סָבְבוּ are formed from סַב ; and how all the other persons of the praeter follow the form of סָבוֹתָ. only three forms are necessary to be specially noted, in order to obtain a view of the whole praeter tense. If the learner is further led to see how verbs of all classes resemble each other, and follow the same general analogy in their inflections, the number of paradigms will cease to be an object of dread with him. The analogical arrangement of these verbs in the paradigms, will render the similarity of them apparent to him, and render it more easy to impress the whole upon his memory ; inasmuch as he will be accustomed to find the same forms in the same place of the paradigm, or if the forms are different, he will be able to compare them with facility, and in doubtful cases to find what he needs.

In the same manner, (but before the verbs with quiescent letters are taken up,) should the verbs which have guttural letters in them be learned, in connexion with the rules that respect the gutturals.

With the preceding exercises, must necessarily be connected *reading and translating ;* in which the teacher, at the commencement, and before the pupil has acquired any skill to pursue the investigation of the words which occur, may for a little while dictate, and direct that what he says should be written down. In doing this, he will have opportunity to say what is necessary respecting the article, particles, the construct state, &c, and to exercise his pupils in the principles which pertain to these things, by making a practical application of the instances which occur. *Let the teacher be careful, that his pupil learn to read with facility, without any hesitating, stuttering, or stammering;* which with some is easy, and soon accomplished; with others, a more difficult task, and slowly performed. The best means for the student, in order to accomplish this, is, *to read* OFTEN *and* ALOUD *those passages which he understands.*

For further exercises in the irregular verbs, I should *specially recommend, that the student be accustomed to form paradigms himself, after the example of those in his grammar, by choosing words which belong to the respective classes of these verbs, and writing out complete paradigms solely by his own efforts.* To these may be added paradigms of verbs specially irregular, and which are not exhibited in the grammar, but may be formed from the rules which it contains. Such, for example, are the verbs בוֹא, עָלָה, &c. *Paradigms should likewise be written out, consisting merely of afformatives, praeformatives, and characteristics of the conjugations.* In doing this, the student must necessarily consult the principles of his grammar very frequently, contract a familiarity with them, and learn to penetrate more deeply into the construction of the language.

The teacher should also give him examples of forms belonging to all the classes of irregular verbs, describe to him the distinctive marks of the several conjugations, and of the different classes of verbs, and then proceed gradually to the anomalous and peculiar forms in each; so that the student may gradually imbibe the spirit of oriental idiom.

As soon as the student acquires skill enough to find words, let the lexicon be put into his hand, and NO TRANSLATION PERMITTED TO BE USED; much less a *Clavis*, as it is called, which takes away all excitement to investigate the sense of words by his own exertions; and moreover will be of serious disadvantage, on account of the meagre account of the meaning of words, which books of this kind contain. The words, especially the more common roots, the student must, at the very outset, engrave upon his memory, in respect both to their original and derived signification; for nothing is more wearisome, or discouraging, than from the defective knowledge of words, to be obliged continually to recur to the lexicon, and reinvestigate again and again.

The use of an accurate translation may, by and by, be permitted and even recommended, at cursory private lectures ; which, however, rather belong to universities than to schools. Such a version may help to ascertain the right sense of difficult passages ; and may serve to recall to mind the meaning of many words, which are but indistinctly impressed upon it, without the trouble of looking them out again in the lexicon.

The reading of the syntax may be left with most students, without any oral instruction from the teacher ; for as progress is made in study, the whole of it must necessarily be adverted to ; and it should be made the *duty of the pupil to go* FULLY *into the oriental idiom,* IN EVERY RESPECT, *so that all parts of the grammar must come to be used.*

This leads us to another point. Every reflecting teacher must know, from his own experience, how much familiarity with *one* particular elementary book, *which unites fulness with precision,* contributes to lead him in the safest and shortest way to that established knowledge, which it is the object of all instruction to convey. On the other hand, he will easily see *how much loss of time, and embarrassment to the student, is occasioned by a change of his elementary books of instruction.*

It is this view of the subject, which has induced me to comprise in the following grammar, although designed for beginners, nearly a complete view of all the grammatical phases of words. It will be necessary, no doubt, for the teacher, at the outset to guide his pupil in the investigation of the anomalies and specialties of the language, which are contained in the notes of his grammar. But the pupil should not be necessitated, with trouble and loss of time, to go to other helps besides his mere skeleton of a grammar, in order to search out the explanation of what he needs.

For the reason just given, *I must protest against the teacher's directing his pupil to the use of a skeleton-grammar, before he takes up this ; or to give him such an one, by dictating so that he may write it out.* This latter method occasions great loss of time ; and besides, it destroys the unity of grammatical system.

It will be a very useful exercise, as the student advances, to put him to translating from his vernacular tongue back into the Hebrew. The teacher may repeat a sentence, or a part of one, in his vernacular language, and then the student may give the corresponding Hebrew. The reading and pointing with the pen an unpointed Hebrew text, is of very great utility, in learning the doctrine of the Hebrew forms. Finally, the student should be accustomed to compose small pieces in Hebrew, which will teach him syntax and the doctrine of forms at the same time. For this purpose, parables in the New Testament, or sententious maxims out of Sirach may be chosen ; the language of which is Hebrew, in its essential idiom, and a part of which was originally composed in Hebrew. In correcting these exercises, the teacher will have a good opportunity to remark on the characteristics of the Hebrew idiom. As useful helps for this purpose, are to be recommended, *Weckherlin's Materials for translating out of the German into the Hebrew language*, Stuttgard, 1812. Also, the *Hebrew Version of the New Testament, lately published by the London Society for promoting Christianity among the Jews*, London, 1817. 8vo.

In regard to the order of studying Hebrew at the schools ; it is a common practice to put boys of the third class to this study, and to let them continue it through the remainder of their course, but only occasionally, i. e. one or two hours in a week. This is a very bad method ; for instruction so seldom imparted makes but little impression, and no rapid progress can possibly be made. In this way, all the excitement and pleasure of studying is removed ; and no zeal for it can be expected. The scholar forgets, by the time when the next lecture comes, what he had learned at the preceding one. It is much better to proceed in Hebrew, as in Latin and Greek ; to lay well the foundation at first, and from the commencement, to devote at least three lectures in a week to it, both for the sake of exciting an interest in the study, and of speedily passing through the elementary stages of acquisition.

PART III.

EXTRACT FROM WYTTENBACH.

I must now say something of the *preparation* of your exercises; in which, if your lexicons lead you into any mistakes, I shall correct them in your recitations. Now at my lectures, you will not be silent hearers only; but you will be called upon to interpret passages of an author, and to answer such questions as I shall put to you. No one of you will fail to do this, who is desirous of making a proficiency in his studies; and of that, you will be desirous. In this way we shall reap the benefit of the Socratic method of instruction; while I shall, at the same time, discover the genius of each one of you, and be enabled to accommodate myself to it. I shall draw out from you all your opinions, both true and false; the former I shall confirm, and the latter will be eradicated. Every day's task will be first gone over by the elder pupils; on the succeeding day, the younger ones will repeat it; and by this method we shall obtain such a familiar acquaintance with an author, that there will be no need of further repetition, but all the pupils will be able to interpret an author together. This is *your* duty. As for *mine*, it consists of so many particulars, that it would be endless to enumerate them; for it comprehends every thing which appertains to accurate interpretation; and as you will learn them all by actual experience, it is unnecessary, and might appear ostentatious in me, to dwell upon them in this place. To sum up the whole in a few words;—it is my endeavour to unite the useful with the agreeable, and in explaining authors, to imbue your minds with a just sense of their real beauties, and by the very pleasure of these exercises, to lead you up to the principles of the language and composition of the Greeks, as they are to be traced either in single words by means of etymologies and analogies, or as they are settled by usage in the construction of sentences.

After this part of your duty comes the task of *repetition* or *reviewing* your studies. This is twofold ; first, on the part of the master (which it is unnecessary here to explain) ; and secondly, on the part of the scholar. *This latter is to be continually practised at home, and* HAS AN INCREDIBLE EFFECT IN ASSISTING YOUR PROGRESS ; *but it must be a* REAL *and* THOROUGH *review ; that is, it must be* AGAIN *and* AGAIN *repeated. What I choose is this ; that every day the task of the preceding day should be reviewed ; at the end of every week, the task of the week ; at the end of every month, the studies of the month ; in addition to which, this whole course should be gone over again during the vacations ;* for the review which is thus made in the vacations, being done more deliberately, is of the utmost efficacy in making you thorough scholars, and affords, besides, the greatest satisfaction by making you sensible of your own proficiency, and inciting you to persevere in your studies. For this reason, I have ever been struck with the good sense of our ancestors (among other things) in appointing vacations ; which were intended by them to give opportunity to the professor for recreation of body and mind, and to the pupils for reviewing their studies. Therefore, my estimable young friends, employ yourselves in the exercise of reviewing, and thus carry into effect the intentions of your wise ancestors. Having then, during the vacation, gone over the whole of your preceding studies, you will anticipate and be prepared to meet those of the succeeding year ; such of you, I mean, as shall again return to your studies in Greek literature. Nor will those of you, who may leave me and return home, wholly neglect in private the pursuit of this or any other part of learning, and thus consign to oblivion all your acquisitions. On the contrary, you will not fail to devote one hour or part of an hour at least, every day, to these studies, on the same plan which you have followed under me ; *for there is no business of life, no avocation whatever, which will not permit a man,* WHO HAS AN INCLINATION, *to give a little time every day to the studies of his youth.* And in case you faithfully keep up this practice of reviewing your Greek studies, I shall, in truth, be the most empty of all boasters, if you do not in a short time acquire such a familiarity with the language, that you will be able to read Greek with just the same facility as Latin authors, or even the writers in any modern language with which you are acquainted. I can truly say, that if I have made any progress myself in Greek learning, I owe it to this practice of reviewing.

It will not be out of place here, to give you some account of my own studies ; for perhaps you may be incited by my example. When I was in my eighteenth year, I had learned about as much Greek, as you generally know, after being with me four months. I diligently attended the professors, both in literature, and in the more profound parts of knowledge, as we are accustomed to speak ; but all, with very little advantage. I appeared indeed to others to have made some progress, but I did not feel sensible of it myself ; I repented of my labour, and looked around for room to take a higher flight. I returned to my studies, and determined to go over them again under the guidance of my own feelings. I did so ; and indeed advanced in this way somewhat farther than I had done during the period of my attending the professors ; but still I accomplished nothing in comparison with my expectations, and I gave up the whole in disgust. I then went from one study to another, but they were all alike repulsive and irksome ; and yet, like one whose appetite is disordered, I was constantly seeking for some intellectual nutriment. I at length recollected the pleasure which I took, when a boy, in the study of Greek, and I began to look round for some book that I had formerly read. I took down from my shelves the little work of Plutarch on the Education of Children, and read it once. I then went through it a second time. This was truly a task, and was far from affording me any pleasure. From

Plutarch I betook myself to Herodian, which gave me rather more pleasure, but still did not satisfy me. Then, as by chance, I met with a copy of Ernesti's edition of the Memorabilia of Xenophon, an author whom I had as yet known merely by name; and I was wonderfully captivated with the indescribable suavity of that author; and yet I was not so fully sensible of his excellence at this time, as I was afterwards. In reading and studying this work, I made it a rule never to begin a section without re-perusing the preceding one; nor a chapter nor book, without going over the preceding chapter and book a second time; and finally, after having finished the work in that manner, I again read the whole in course. This was a labour of almost three months; but such constant repetition proved most beneficial to me. The effect of repetition seemed to be, that when I proceeded from a section or chapter, which I had read twice, to a new one, I acquired an impulse which bore me along through all opposing obstacles; like a vessel, (to use Cicero's comparison in a similar case,) which having once received an impulse from the oar, continues on her course even after the mariners have suspended their exertions to propel her.

I have therefore constantly adhered to this practice of repeating or reviewing. After having thus acquired some knowledge of the Greek language, and by means of Ernesti's short notes become acquainted in some measure with the principles of interpretation as well as with books, I resolved to devote myself to Greek literature; and from that time I commenced the reading of the Greek authors. I began with Homer's Iliad, of which, while a boy, I had read about an hundred lines in the first book. I read it at this time in the same manner as I had done Xenophon's Memorabilia,—that is, continually repeating each portion that I studied; and I finished the whole in two months. I regretted that I had used Schrevelius; for by following him, I was led into very many errors, to correct which afterwards cost me much time and labour. Oh! that I had then known and enjoyed the benefit of being directed by the light of the Hemsterhusian method, which is now enjoyed in the schools of Holland and is accessible to you; and so much the more sure you may now be of making a proficiency in your studies, as your advantages are greater than mine were in my youth. But to return.

I proceeded with Homer, rather because it was necessary than because I found it agreeable ; for I was not yet sensible of the powers of that divine poet. I have known other young persons experience the same thing; the cause of which I afterwards understood, but it would be tiresome here to explain it at large. I therefore took up Xenophon in conjunction with Homer, and gave the greatest portion of my time to his works, which I almost devoured ; so easy were they to me, that I was rarely obliged to use a lexicon, for every thing was intelligible from the connexion of the sentence. I had, moreover, a Latin translation, which was of use to me at my age, but never is to boys at school. I thus went through all the works of Xenophon (except the Memorabilia) four times in four months. I now began to think there was no author that would not be easy to me ; and I took up Demosthenes. I had an edition with the Greek text only, accompanied with the Greek notes of Wolfius. Alas! darkness itself! But I had learned not to be deterred on the first approach, and I persevered. I found greater difficulties than ever, both in the words and in the extent of the orator's propositions; but, at last, after much labour I reached the end of the first Olynthiac. I then read it a second and third time, when every thing appeared clear, but still I found nothing of those powers of eloquence of which we hear so much. I doubted at this time whether I should venture upon another of his orations, or should review again the one which I had just read ; I decided however to review it; and (how wonderful are the effects of this practice, which can never be sufficiently recommended !) as I read, a new and unknown feeling took possession of my mind. Hitherto in reading the Greek authors, I had experienced only that pleasure which arose from understanding their meaning and the subjects discussed by them, and from observing my own proficiency. But in reading Demosthenes, an unusual and more than human emotion pervaded my mind, and grew stronger upon every successive perusal. I could now see the orator at one time all ardour; at another, in anguish ; and at another, borne away by an impulse which nothing could resist. As I proceed, the same ardour begins to be kindled within myself, and I am carried away by the same impulse. I feel a greater elevation of soul, and am no longer the same man. I fancy that I am Demosthenes himself standing before the assembly, delivering this oration, and exhorting the Athenians to emulate the bravery and the glory of their ancestors; and now, I can no longer read the oration silently, as at first, but aloud; to which I am insensibly impelled, by the strength and fervour of the sentiments as well as by the power of oratorical harmony.

Pursuing this method, I read almost all the orations of Demosthenes in the course of three months; and by this means being the better qualified to understand the Grecian writers, I was more than ever delighted with Homer, and soon finished reading him; after which I employed myself more advantageously upon other authors. The next I began was Plato, with whose works I am persuaded I never should have been so much captivated, if I had not brought to them an ardour, which was ever the more ready to kindle in consequence of the excitement produced by the study of Demosthenes. There is, indeed, in Plato an exuberance and force of genius, tempered with a certain sedateness, yet diversified as well as inexhaustible, which cannot fail to soften and move the most inflexible reader. In Xenophon, it is true, we see a perfect and highly wrought picture of Socrates; yet it is but a picture. But in Plato we see Socrates himself in every thing except his material form; he lives, breathes, speaks and acts; and invites the reader to participate with him in all he does. I should add, that I was wonderfully aided in understanding him by Ruhnken's observations on Timæus's lexicon, from which I derived all that light which enabled me to perceive the powerful influence of Plato's genius throughout the world of letters. After this I proceeded to all the other classic authors of the first rank, and the philosophers and sophists of the later periods; not omitting even those of the fathers, whose writings were connected with ancient learning. This whole course of reading, from the time I began Xenophon's Memorabilia, was accomplished in four years; and I gave an account of it in a letter to Ruhnken, informing him that he had, though without knowing me, been a guide to me in a most efficacious and sure method of study.

NOTES

BY THE TRANSLATOR.

NOTE A. page 9.

The reader will bear in mind, that the authorised version in the Romish church, with which Jahn is connected, is the Vulgate or Latin translation of the Scriptures, made by Jerome about the beginning of the fifth century. This, although made from the original Hebrew Scriptures by the best oriental scholar among all the ancient fathers, and giving, on the whole, a more complete view of their meaning than any other ancient version, is less able and faithful than our common English translation. Jahn might, therefore, say what he does in regard to that version, with more reason than we can say the same thing of ours. Indeed, ours is, on the whole, a most noble production for the time in which it was made. The divines of that day were very different Hebrew scholars from what most of their successors have been, in England or Scotland. With the exception of Bishop Lowth's classic work upon Isaiah, no other effort at translating, among the English divines, will compare either in respect to taste, judgment, or sound understanding of the Hebrew, with our authorised version.

After all, can it be supposed, from the nature of the case, that a single effort exhausted all the powers of the human mind upon the Hebrew text, and left no chance for improvement in after ages ? In what branch of human knowledge has this ever been the case ? A person well acquainted with the history of oriental study must know, that very many sources of knowledge have been opened within the last half century, which were closed before. The consequence has been, that a great number of difficult and doubtful texts have been illustrated, which before were obscure, or unintelligible. Let a person well acquainted with the present state of Hebrew philology, read the book of Job, (a very difficult book to translate in an adequate manner,) and compare it with our version, and he will find frequent reason to apply what Jahn has said of the Vulgate to our own translation.

NOTE B. page 10.

To relieve the difficulty which some minds may feel, in consequence of such a representation as that which is contained in the view given by Jahn of versions, and in the preceding note, it may safely be asserted, that the worst translation which was ever made of the Scriptures, contains *all that is essential to salvation*, either as it respects doctrine or practice. Some translations have added things to the Scriptures, which religion does not require ; and some have made one part of the Bible to gainsay another part. But the worst translation never removed, nor wholly obscured, the great and leading principles of revealed religion.

The difference then between a version of the better and poorer sort, is not that the latter is *insufficient* for the purposes of *personal salvation*, and the former *sufficient ;* but that the former, in a much better manner than the latter, enables the " man of God to become more perfect in Christian knowledge, and *more thoroughly* furnished unto every good work." In a word, if what the sacred writers have said is important, and *all* of it is important, it is desirable to understand *all* which they have said ; and the more perfect a translation is, the better will Christians be able to gain this knowledge. I may be saved, possibly, if I never become acquainted with ten thousand shades of thought, which the *original* Scriptures convey, and which do not appear in any translation that I read ; but I may love the Scriptures more, (if I have a right temper of mind,) and understand them better, when all those divine beauties, which are obscured by a translation, are fully unfolded to my view.

NOTE C. page 10.

Near the commencement of the third century, the variations from each other of the Greek versions then extant, and the ever varying copies of the Septuagint version itself, and its numerous and manifest departures from the Hebrew, excited Origen to undertake the compilation of the great work, which is commonly denominated the *Hexapla.* His object in doing this was, to compare the Septuagint with the original Hebrew, and with all the other Greek versions, in order to establish the text of the Septuagint, and secure it against future innovations ; and also to furnish others with the obvious means of making the same comparison. He is said to have devoted twenty eight years to the compilation of this work. He visited different countries to procure manuscripts of all kinds; and about A. D. 231, fixed upon Cesarea as his place of residence. Here he prosecuted his labours; and had in his employ seven ready scribes, exclusively of several females who were skilled in calligraphy. The expense was defrayed by *Ambrosius;* a Maecaenas truly worthy of immortal memory!

The result of these arrangements and labours was the production of the great work in question; which the ancient writers sometimes call *Tetrapla*, sometimes *Hexapla, Octapla* and *Enneapla.* There is great obscurity in many of the accounts of ancient writers with regard to this subject; some appearing to speak as if these, or some of these, were separate works. But, comparing all the accounts together, it seems quite probable, or nearly certain, that these names were given only in reference to separate parts of the work. The whole was written in the manner of a *harmony*, in columns on the same page. The first column was occupied by the original Hebrew; the second, by the Hebrew sounds or words represented in Greek characters; the third by the version of Aquila, as being most literal; the fourth, by that of Symmachus, as rendering *ad sensum* rather than *ad literam;* the fifth, by the Septuagint; the sixth, by the version of Theodotian. These made six columns; whence the Greek denomination *Hexapla*, which means *six-fold*, or *in six columns.* Sometimes two or three anonymous versions were added, of some books or parts of books, which gave rise to the names *Octapla* (eight columns,) and *Enneapla* (nine columns). In some parts, it would seem that two of the *Hexapla* columns must have failed, which gave rise to the name *Tetrapla.*

To the Septuagint version were appended marks, which designated when any thing was added, or subtracted, or changed, in consequence of comparison with the Hebrew, or with the versions.

The enormous expense of such a Polyglott prevented its ever being copied afterwards. It was left by Origen at Tyre; and fifty *years after his death,* (O tempora!) it was found in an *obscure* corner, by Eusebius and Pamphilus, and deposited by the latter in the library at Cesarea. There Jerome found it near the close of the fourth century; and (as no Christian father after him makes any mention of it) there it probably perished in the flames that were kindled by the Arabians, when they took possession of that city in

A. D. 653. How many books of amatory songs and philosophical jargon, which the curiosity of lust and speculation has carefully preserved and transmitted to us from ancient times, might we well spare to redeem such a treasure ! And the Arabians too, (afterwards indeed the patrons of learning, but then) the infuriate votaries of Mohammedan delusion ! If I could find it in my heart to wage a war of extermination with any human beings, it would be with those barbarians, who with relentless fury sacrifice the most precious treasures, which the labours of the greatest minds have been for ages in collecting, and which are designed to enrich the whole race of man ; and sacrifice them too, without even a prospect of promoting in any possible manner their own interest or glory by it, and with the insult of contempt. Hos, Dii execrantur ! Hos, boni omnes maledicunt.

A thousand questions in criticism, which now agitate the Christian world, and will continue to do so for years to come, could all be settled in a moment, by appeal to this work of Origen. But it is gone ! And though the immortal critic is not robbed of his glory, this is of little consequence and little avail to the church, who need the result of his labours more than the praise which is bestowed on him. All that remains are mere fragments, collected by Montfaucon and others, which do little more than serve to show us what we have lost. I would barter all that the ruins of Herculaneum, and the pyramids and mausoleums of Egypt have ever afforded, or ever will afford, for this one volume of Origen. But peace ! Complaint is unavailing and improper. חָפֵץ יְהֹוָה יַעֲשֶׂה כַּאֲשֶׁר טוֹב בְּעֵינָיו.

Note D. page 14.

Jahn here employs the word *critical* in the *limited* sense, in which it was fashionable for a while among many of the Literati on the continent of Europe to use it ; viz. as indicating merely that kind of labour and judgment, which is employed in settling the genuineness of any author's text, or parts of the same. But general usage now employs the word in a much more extensive sense, viz, to indicate any kind of labour or judgment employed in settling the text itself, explaining it, or giving the literary history of it. The former is called by the Germans *lower criticism*, and is very rightly named, for the most part ; the latter *higher criticism*, because the objects and results of it are of a more important nature.

I have intimated, that criticism on the various readings of the text of any author is very properly denominated " lower criticism." I would not be understood, however, to speak with any disrespect of those industrious and very useful men, who have laboured in this department of sacred literature. Such are Kennicott, De Rossi, Bruns, Mill, Wetstein, Bengel, Griesbach, Matthiæ, Birch, Alter, and many others. Some of these were men of very extensive erudition. Nor would I be understood as intimating, that it is of little importance, whether we strive to attain a pure Hebrew and Greek text of the Scriptures. This is important, just in proportion to the value of the books themselves. But most who are well versed in sacred literature, will now, I believe, readily acknowledge that the importance of labors in this department were greatly overvalued, some thirty or twenty years since, and that a great deal too much was expected from them. When Kennicott undertook his great work of comparing several hundred Hebrew manuscripts and editions, fifty years ago, all Europe was placed in the attitude of anxious expectation. One party who held, (as Buxtorf long before had asserted,) that all the Hebrew manuscripts, the world over, were to a point and accent exactly the same, stood waiting ; alternately agitated by the hope that the result would prove to be so, and the fear that it might turn out differently. Another party, who had been perpetually carping at the Hebrew text, accusing the Jews of having mutilated and interpolated it, and guessing what it *should* be, rather than learning to explain what it *was*, most eagerly expected a complete triumph over their opponents who had fought against this conjectural criticism, and doubted not that all the anomalies of Hebrew grammar, and all the dark and difficult places of the Scripture, would be thrown out.

Both were egregiously disappointed in the result. On the one hand, the various readings amounted to several hundred thousands ; no two manuscripts, or copies being found which did not differ from each other in a multitude of places : on the other hand, not the one hundredth part of all this immense mass of various readings amounted, in point of importance, to any thing more, than the question whether the word *honour* should be spelled with or without the letter *U*. One might, indeed, if the subject were not in itself of too serious a nature, be tempted to apply to the result the well known adage of Horace, *Parturiunt montes* &c.

De Rossi added to the labours of Kennicott, the comparison of a still greater number of manuscripts and editions. This veteran in Hebrew literature is still living, and has distinguished himself by a multitude of useful publications relative to the Hebrew language and Jewish writers.

Both Kennicott and De Rossi laid down a considerable number of rules, by which the age and value of Hebrew manuscripts are to be ascertained. These cannot be cited, much less discussed here. Suffice it to say, that succeeding critics (Tychsen, Eichhorn, and others) have discussed these rules, and shown, that nearly every ground of distinction which Kennicott and De Rossi had laid down, is fallacious ; and, of course, that very little dependence can be placed on their estimate of the value of any *various reading.*

The consequence has been, that although the great works of these collators, accomplished by incredible labour and diligence, are found in most libraries designed for theological use, yet they are consulted and regarded in a very moderate degree. The best interpreters of the Old Testament scarcely mention them in their commentaries ; and the high hopes which were entertained about them have sunk into disappointment, and of course are succeeded by a great degree of neglect.

Time was, when the collation of Hebrew manuscripts was regarded as the highest object of criticism. The time now has come, when scarcely any one takes an interest in it. Such great changes does time make in respect to subjects of criticism, when they are amply discussed and examined. We may apply to all subjects of this nature, the beautiful saying which Jahn has quoted from Aulus Gellius ; *Truth is the daughter of time.*

In regard to the New Testament, somewhat more has been accomplished; but very much, which it was once expected would be done, still remains unaccomplished. The labours of former critics, Mill, Wetstein, and Bengel, though not useless, have been in a great measure superseded by those of recent ones, Griesbach, Matthiæ and others. But Griesbach differs very much, as to many of his maxims in respect to judging of the genuineness of the text, from Matthiæ ; and though his work has become so popular in England and in this country, yet the critics of Germany are not by any means unanimous in receiving it throughout ; many siding partially with Matthiæ, and others (some of the most eminent ones) choosing a middle path between him and Griesbach. In England, Dr. Lawrence has, in a very able Tract, recently called in question the fundamental maxims of classifying manuscripts, on which Griesbach relies as being most important in judging of their weight and authority, with a view to decide questions concerning the text of the New Testament.

Lower criticism then, after all, has won much less ground, than many departments of sacred literature. Many very important facts it has brought to light. But the proper mode of reasoning from these, or the deductions which in a variety of respects are to be made as to many important points, remain yet unsettled.

No biblical student should be ignorant of the history and state of *lower criticism.* But Jahn has given it, (as was the mode, when he wrote the dissertation on which I am commenting,) a higher place than can well be assigned to it, until the science becomes more definite, established, and satisfactory. The subject is of unquestionable importance, and that in a high degree. But what I aim at saying is, that sufficient light has not yet been cast upon it, to make it so valuable to a critic and theologian, as many other subjects of criticism are. More labour, more comparison of manuscripts, more discussion in regard to the rules of estimating their worth, and a more thorough development of the internal characteristics of every sacred writer's style, are necessary, before the student can realize a very fruitful harvest from this field.

What Eichhorn said long ago, when remarking on the changes which bishop Lowth had made in the text of Isaiah, appears to me very judicious and strictly correct; viz, *that the better any one understands the Hebrew text, the less will he feel the need of emendations, and the less probable will they appear;* a maxim which I could wish he and many others might have always remembered. There is no ancient book on earth, which has such and so many vouchers for an uncontaminated text, in general, as the Old Testament. Of course, less is to be expected, and less is needed from the labours of lower criticism, than in regard to any other ancient book.

--••●●••--

NOTE E. page 17.

It. is very probable, that the view which Jahn has taken of this subject, may appear to many, who read these pages, to be too highly colored. It is natural however for men of ardent feelings, and who have known by experience how much they themselves have been prof-

ited by such studies, to draw in strong colors the picture of their utility. And if our author has done this, we may easily pardon him, con-
sidering the opposition which he met with from ecclesiastics in the
pale of the Romish church, many of whom are strongly opposed to
general and thorough investigation of the Scriptures.

It is quite needless for me to repeat here what has been suggested, to show the utility and importance of sacred philology. But if
the patience of the reader will permit, and I may venture to hope that
I shall not be charged with assuming too much, I will endeavour to
state, in a plain and brief manner, my view of this subject.

1st. No translation is or ever was made by inspired men ; none
therefore is secure, in all respects, from the effect of human frailty
and error. The original Scriptures then are, and always must be,
the only *ultimate* and *highest* source of appeal, to establish any sentiment pertaining to doctrine or practice. Such has been the grand
maxim of the most learned Protestants, in all their disputes with the
Romish church.

2dly. All revealed religion, or *biblical theology* depends solely on
what is contained in the Scriptures. "The Bible is the *only* and
sufficient rule of faith and practice." What this says is orthodoxy ;
and what this does not say, or plainly imply, is not necessary to our
faith or our practice. Of course, the ultimate appeal, on every
point in theology, is to the declarations of the Scripture. It matters
not to the unprejudiced inquirer, what writers or preachers have inculcated as theology, if it be not supported by the word of God. But,

3dly. Who is in the best situation to make and judge of the appeal
in question, which for the reason above stated must always be ultimately made to the *original* Scriptures ? The man who does not understand them, or the man who does ? And is it not desirable that a
teacher of religion should be able, in case of dispute, or where he
wishes to satisfy his own mind, to make the *highest* appeal which can
be made to the book on whose decisions he depends for support ?

This contains a summary view of the most important point. Let
me add, in a miscellaneous way, several considerations.

Commentaries on the original can neither be well understood, nor
well judged of, without a knowledge of the original itself. The same
thing may be said of critical dissertations ; and of all systematic theology, which is built simply upon the Scriptures.

The extensive reading and study, which the knowledge in ques-

tion requires, must enlarge every man's mind, who embarks heartily
in it. The Bible, in such a course of study, becomes the central point
to which all his exertions are directed ; and should not this be the
case, with a Christian minister ?

Let it not be said, that after all we are obliged to depend on the
opinions of critics and lexicographers, for the meaning of the originals, and so with all this toil, we can at last acquire but *secondary*
knowledge. This is no more true, than that we depend on Johnson's
dictionary for the understanding of an English sentence. While we
are tyros in Greek and Hebrew, what is alleged may apply ; just
as children depend on those who are around them for the meaning of
words, when they are learning to talk. But by and by, they come
to reason in the same way to prove what the meaning of words is, as
Johnson did in compiling his dictionary. And so it is with the thorough Greek and Hebrew scholar. He can make his own lexicon and
grammar.

Most of the objections brought against the study of these languages
are so copiously discussed by Jahn, in a succeeding part of his dissertation, that it is unnecessary for me to canvass them. Instead of
doing this, I shall now say a few things, which justice requires to be
said, in regard to those religious teachers, who are unacquainted, or
but very slightly acquainted, with the original Scriptures.

What candid man will deny that there have been, and now are,
many excellent men of this class endowed with great powers of
mind, men of exalted Christian attainments, and of high worth in the
church ? Men too, who have far excelled, in almost every proper
and useful qualification of a Christian minister, multitudes of others
that have spent years in the study of Greek and Hebrew. One
must be ignorant of the history of the church, or of the character of
its ministers, who will not very readily accede to this ; for it would
be easy to fill pages with the names of men, living and dead, belonging to this class, whose characters shine as stars in the firmament.

But on the other hand ; supposing these same men, had added to
all their excellent endowments a profound knowledge of the original Scriptures ; might they not have been brighter ornaments still
to the Christian church ? KNOWLEDGE IS POWER; and knowledge of
the Scriptures is power of a very important nature, to a man whose
business it is to teach what the Scriptures inculcate. Might not
their influence have been more widely diffused still, if they had been

extensively versed in *all* which pertains to the illustration of the sacred volume ?

This is the fair state of the question. The inquiry is not whether men have been useful ministers, who were not good linguists. No one in his senses can undertake to deny this.

In deliberating, then, whether a candidate for the ministry shall study the original Scriptures, the only point which need to be debated is, whether he shall content himself with a less measure of utility, instead of aiming to attain a greater one. Would God that a high sense of Christian duty, and a noble enthusiasm to be useful, might ever decide this question; which alas ! is so often decided by timidity, and above all by the love of ease, by the want of energetic decision of character, by devotedness to worldly cares, and by vague and incompetent views of the utility of the studies in question. Many are contented, if they can attain to a mere modicum of respectability ; and quietly sit down with the intention to lean upon what others have done, and depend on their *authority*, rather than on the *reason* of the case, whenever a philological question occurs.

The time has been, it must be acknowledged, when in our country, scarcely any degree of ardour for Biblical study could have overcome the difficulties which stood in the way. There were no schools, no books, no teachers to aid in the study of the original Scriptures. These difficulties are vanishing apace. Hebrew study not only makes a part of the plan of education in all our theological Seminaries, but Hebrew is beginning to be a subject of collegiate attention, and will eventually find its way, I hope and trust, into our higher Schools, and be cultivated by many private individuals, who have a relish for Biblical study. A young man, therefore, who now is entering upon the ministry, can scarcely fail of an opportunity to pursue oriental study, if he chooses to do it ; and consequently he will be inexcusable, in ordinary cases, if he neglects to avail himself of such an opportunity.

Things were not in such a state, when the great body of the ministers of middle age, or more advanced, who are now upon the stage, were educated. These remarks cannot be so applied, as to implicate or find fault with them. Of most of these, it would be altogether out of the usual course of things, to expect that they should commence these studies, even if the means are at hand. The time of some is too short, and others are actively and constantly engaged in the great plans of beneficence, which are now in the course of execution, to reform the Christian and the heathen world. Nor am I such a strenuous advocate for the studies in question, as to maintain that no cases can occur where young men should now be licensed to preach, without the knowledge of them. Does not the church need teachers of all degrees of knowledge? May not ardent piety, united with good sense, inculcate the fundamental principles of religion and be the means of saving multitudes, although it is associated with a very moderate stock of learning? Or even where, *appropriately* speaking, there is no *learning* at all? I answer without hesitation in the affirmative. The church needs in her service officers of all ranks; and soldiers too may surely be employed to a very valuable purpose. Every day's experience shows this, where the trial is made. And thus too did the primitive Christians. " They that were scattered abroad—went every where preaching the word," that is, publishing the doctrines of the gospel. These were not apostles, but Christians of the common rank, Acts viii. 1—4. I should not hesitate a moment about the expediency of employing pious men of all degrees of knowledge, *to teach what they are adequate to teach.*

But in saying this, I must not be understood as avowing any approbation of unlicensed and unqualified individuals assuming the whole of the *ministerial* office, and administering the sacraments. To encourage this, is dangerous to the peace and good order of the Church. Individuals destitute of a good education, and exalted to such a place in the Church, almost invariably become vain, obtrusive, and uneasy under any restraint or control. They look down with a great deal of contempt upon those poor plodders, who have been obliged to be drilled by colleges, in order to get knowledge enough to know how to open their mouths; while, as to themselves—they have been taught by inspiration, and are the distinguished favorites of heaven. What follows? The regularly educated clergy are first despised; then treated with contumely; then set at defiance. Thus the order of the church is greatly disturbed, and many persons are led away from the path of discretion and humility.

But then, the abuse of lay-service for the good of the Church is no argument against the thing itself, when properly conducted. One simple rule may guide. *Let no one teach, except in that which he is qualified to teach ; and let no one assume the prerogatives of office, until he is regularly invested with the office.*

To return ; shall we not have as many teachers as we can, of the most *enlightened* class ? The general voice of our country is beginning to say—Yes. It is auspicious to the interests of the church. It is gratifying also to see so many of our excellent ministers, who in the season of their education were denied the privileges which young candidates may now enjoy, so warmly recommend and enforce upon our youth a thorough education. How different the state of our country in this respect, as well as in many others, from that which exists among the members of the Romish church, of which, in the sequel, Jahn so loudly complains.!

Two points in respect to the subject in question, are of the highest magnitude. The *first* and *greatest* of all is, that THOSE WHO DEVOTE THEMSELVES TO THE WORK OF THE MINISTRY SHOULD BE POSSESSED OF REAL AND FERVENT PIETY. To enter into the ministry as a *profession* simply, by which a man is to obtain his living, is a most sacrilegious affront to the pure and awful nature of religion. God requires the *heart ;* and the unhappy youth who does not give it to him, who does not enter upon the work of the ministry with sincere devotedness to the interests of religion, and with that singleness of mind which will lead him to be wholly engrossed with this great cause, is condemned to act the hypocrite, as long as he wears the clerical garb ; to dishonour religion by his cold, dull, mere moralizing, speculative manner of preaching ; and to offend God, who is a witness of his hypocrisy and his spiritual sloth. Better would it be for him, and for the church too, that he had lived and died in a heathen land, without the knowledge of salvation.

Luther represented justification by faith as the *articulus stantis vel cadentis ecclesiæ.* I believe in gratuitous justification too ; but I would sooner represent the *article* in question, (certainly as it respects the success and flourishing condition of the Church in the world,) to be *the deep experimental piety of its ministers,* than almost any thing else. All the literary acquisitions on earth can make no compensation for the want of this. "Though I speak with the tongues of men and angels, and have not *love,* I am as sounding brass or a tinkling cymbal."

Indeed a learned ministry, whose hearts are not burning with the flame of devotion *daily* lighted up anew from the altar of God, will probably do incomparably more mischief in the world, than an ignorant ministry of the same moral character ; because their example and their learning will have more influence. The highest curse which can befal the church of God, is, to have its hosts marshalled and directed by men who are secretly hostile to its cause, and at heart in league with the enemy. And very little better than such, as to any good which they will do the church, are men of a temporizing, frigid, speculating, doubtful cast; who, let what topic you please in theology be brought under discussion, always incline to contemplate the objection-side of the question, and can always see ten doubts against a thing, where one good reason can be found in favour of it. Such were not Peter, and Paul, and John, and Stephen. Let such—all such—go to law, physic, classics, farms, merchandise—any thing rather than the ministry. The cause is too high and holy, to be tampered with by secret enemies, or by cold doubting speculators. *Procul, O procul!*

But since I have explained myself so as not to be misunderstood relative to this grand topic, I may now add, that the *second point* to which I meant to refer above, is, that THE CHURCH SHOULD HAVE A LEARNED AS WELL AS A PIOUS MINISTRY. Not that all ministers are to be commentators or lexicographers—but that some are—and as many are to be *qualified* for such undertakings, as the nature of the case will admit. To give the reasons for this, would be to repeat all which has been said in the preceding pages.

A word on objections to the philological study of the Bible.

To say that many divines who have been good linguists were not good pastors, is only saying that a useful talent may be buried, or perverted to bad purposes. Does this prove that the talent is not capable of being employed for *good* and *important* purposes? No doubt, a man who studies the languages may have very little grace, or none at all; and may not this be the case with some, who do not study them? He may be vain of his acquisitions, and lug in his quotations of Greek and Hebrew on every occasion, for the sake of ostentation, and to show his superiority to others; but such a man is not made a silly coxcomb by Greek and Hebrew. They only afford him one of the means, by which he displays the folly and vanity of his own conceited heart.

In a word, if you require only so much knowledge of a minister, as is necessary to his own personal salvation, or to state simply what is *necessary* to the salvation of his flock, you may dispense with a liberal, and even an academic education. But if he is to become a
10

" scribe well instructed in things pertaining to the kingdom of heaven," and " to bring out of his treasure things new and old," the more he studies his *Bible*, the better.   This is the only legitimate source of all true theology.   And in this sacred volume lie hidden numberless glories, which no translation can ever unfold.   I grant that these are not essential to salvation.   I bless God that they are not ; for how then could the great mass of people be saved ?   But may not the contemplation of them help to cultivate a finer taste, and a higher relish in a Christian minister for the sacred word ?   Will it not lead him to pore over its pages with a keener relish, than the most enthusiastic admirers of Greek or Roman poetry have ever entertained for the works of Homer or Virgil ?   I hesitate not to answer in the affirmative.   And if his heart is in any good measure as it ought to be— humble, filial, " panting after God"—by the contemplation of these divine beauties he will be " transformed from glory to glory," as by the Spirit of the living God.

It may be proper to conclude this note, by subjoining the sentiments of some of the most distinguished Protestants, in relation to the importance of Hebrew study, while they were fighting the battles of the Reformation.

MELANCTHON.   " Scio me vix primis labiis degustasse litteras Latinas, Græcas, et Ebraicas.   Sed tamen hoc ipsum, quod didici, quantulumcunque est, propter judicium de Religione, OMNIBUS MUNDI REGNIS OMNIUMQUE OPIBUS LONGE ANTEPONO."

" Est nostri officii juventutem adhortari, ut hoc donum *(linguæ Hebrææ)* quod Deus semper in Ecclesia excitavit, et studiis doctorum conservari voluit, tueantur ac sciant se laborem sumere in MUNERE DIVINO PROPAGANDO, ET IN VERIS ECCLESIÆ OPIBUS DEFENDENDIS."

" De linguæ hujus studio hoc vos oro et obtestor, ut cogitetis donum linguarum in Ecclesia divinitus excitari ; et velle Deum, ut NOSTRA DILIGENTIA ID MUNUS TUEAMUR.   Et laudat servos, qui talenta collocarant in fœnus ; et minatur ignavis, inquiens : Habenti dabitur ; et non habenti, etiam id quod videtur habere, auferetur." (Opp. Tom. III. p. 812. 821, et *ad finem Orat.*)

" Necesse est in Ecclesia conservari linguæ Ebræe cognitionem, cum et Prophetarum libri Ebræi sint, et Apostolica phrasis magna ex parte Ebræa sit.—Nec dubium est semper in Ecclesia aliquos fuisse ejus linguæ gnaros ; etsi enim extant interpretationes necessariæ populo, et profecto non contemnendæ, tamen Deus semper vult tes-

tes aliquos illarum interpretationum esse. Vult in locis obscuris consuli fontes. Id beneficium Dei cognoscamus, et læti ac grati hanc linguam discamus, et QUAM PLURIMOS AD EAM DISCENDAM INVITEMUS."

" Quanto fit illustrior sententia Prophetarum iis, qui fontes norunt, experti judicare possunt. Illud constat, VALDE DELECTARI BONAS MENTES CERTITUDINE SENTENTIÆ, cum nota sit prophetarum lingua."

" Hieronymum adfirmo optime meritum esse, quod Prophetica scripta Latine reddidit. Bene meriti sunt et Septuaginta, aut quicunque alii fuerint, qui Græce reddiderunt. Sed tamen in utraque interpretatione multa esse mendosa, plurima obscura, manifestum est. NECESSARIA EST IGITUR EX FONTIBUS EMENDATIO." *(Monitum Lectori praefixum Avenarii Grammaticae Heb.)*

LUTHER. " Scio quantum mihi cognitio linguæ Ebrææ contra meos hostes profuerit. Quare hac quantulacumque cognitione INFINITIS MILIBUS AUREORUM carere nolim."

" Et vos quoque dabitis operam, qui aliquando docebitis religionem, ut hanc linguam discatis, si non pecora campi et indoctum vulgus haberi vultis.—Sæpe monui ut Ebræam linguam disceretis.—Studium quod in hanc linguam discendam collocatur, missa quædam, seu cultus Dei, merito vocari possit. Quare serio vos hortor, ne eam negligatis. Periculum enim est, ne Deus hac ingratitudinè offensus privet nos non solum cognitione hujus sacræ linguæ, sed et Grecæ et Latinæ, et totius religionis."

" Sed præterquam, quod pars cultus divini est hoc studium, continet etiam maximam utilitatem. Si enim aliqui futuri sunt THEOLOGI sicut necesse est, (neque enim omnes Jura et Medicinam discemus,) oportet eos esse munitos contra PAPATUM, et alios, qui cum unam Ebræam vocem sonare didicerunt, statim putant se Magistros hujus sacræ linguæ. Ibi nisi nos eam tenuerimus, tanquam asinis illudent et insultabunt. Sin autem nos quoque muniti fuerimus cognitione hujus linguæ, poterimus eis impudens os obstruere." *(Comment. in* Psalm. xlv.)

SIXTINUS AMAMA. "Aio itaque nullum ministrum, qui linguarum rudis sit, in arenam posse descendere cum docto Papista, Socinianove, nedum os posse obturare adversario, quod tamen Paulus in ministro desiderat. Nulla versio utrinque recepta est; ULTIMUM PRINCIPIUM EST ORIGINALIS TEXTUS." *(Antibarbarus Biblicus).*

" Augustinus jam progressa ælate Græce discebat, et passim dolet sibi non licuisse Ebrææ notitiam addere. Cum autem intelligeret

quantus sibi frustrationes afferat ejus ignorantia, hortatur omnes
Scripturæ studiosos ne ullam ejus discendæ occasionem negligant."

"Provoco tandem ad conscientias omnium piorum ministrorum, qui
aut præceptorum defectu, aut negligentia, aut denique mala studio-
rum directione has linguas in academiis non didicerunt, annon jam in
sanctissimi muneris functione, et sacrarum litterarum assidua medi-
tatione, agnoscant, quantas sibi frustrationes illarum ignorantia afferat.
—Rogantur itaque per viscera misericordiæ Domini nostri Jesu Christi,
ut CONJUNCTIS OPERIS ID AGANT STRENUE, UT SANCTISSIMA HÆC STUDIA,
TEMPORUM INJURIA PROPEMODUM COLLAPSA, IN ECCLESIA DEI REFLO-
RESCANT." *(Paraenesi)*.

GERHARD. "Miserum est in re tanta alienis videre oculis, eum
præsertim, QUI ALIORUM OCCULUS EST CONSTITUTUS," *(Meth. stud.
Theol)*.

GLASS. "Hebræam linguam si dico, rem dico, quæ omnium vere
Christianorum et mentes et oculos in se convertere, æstimationemque
cum admiratione summa conjunctam concitare, debet et potest.—He-
bræa lingua, quæ mel meum est, meum nectar et ambrosia, meus sco-
pus, mea prora puppisque, &c," *(Orat. de linguaeHebraeae necessitate)*.

I have only to add, that as battles of equal and perhaps greater
moment are now begun, and are still to be fought in order to defend
what the contest of the Reformers won, the above sentiments may
well be addressed to all our young men, who are devoted to the study
of theology.

———

NOTE F. page 18.

The sentiment advanced in this paragraph, is, so far as I know,
uncontroverted by any respectable critic or theologian at present
in the Christian church. All agree, at last, that the apostles and dis-
ciples, who were the writers of the New Testament and belonged to
the Jewish nation, did write in that style of Greek, which is denominated *Hellenistic* or Hebrew Greek, in distinction from *Hellenic*
or Attic Greek. The time has been, however, when multitudes,
nay, the great body of the Christian church, and specially the Protestant part of it, entertained a very different opinion, in regard to this
subject.

Controversy on this topic began, very soon after the revival of
literature in Europe. In the 16th Century, Erasmus and Laurentius
Valla ventured to assert publicly, that the Greek of the New Tes-

tament is Hellenistic. Many learned men of that day were inclined to adopt this opinon. But Robert Stephens, in the preface to his celebrated edition of the New Testament (1576), took it into his head strenuously to contend for the Attic purity of its dialect. As his Testament was so widely circulated, the preface served to excite general attention to the subject in question, and to prepare the minds of critics for the mighty contest which followed.

Sebastian Pforscher led the way, in his *Diatribe de ling. Graec. N. Test. puritate*, published in 1629, at Amsterdam; in which he defends, with great warmth, the purity of the New Testament Greek. His antagonist was J. Jung, who published in 1640 his *Sententiae doctiss. virorum, de Hellenistis et Hellenistica Dialecto.* To this a reply was made, by J. Grosse of Jena, styled *Trias propositionum theol. stilum Nov. Test. a barbaris criminationibus vindicantium;* in which the whole mass of Hellenists were consigned over to the most detestable heresy.

In the same year, Wulfer wrote an answer to this, in his *Innocentia Hellenistarum vindicata;* to which Grosse replied, in his *Observationes pro triade Observatt. apologeticae.* Musaeus defended Wulfer (though not in all his positions) in his *Disquisitio de stilo Nov. Tetamenti,* A. D. 1641 ; to which Grosse replied by a *Tertia defensio Triados,* 1641. In 1642, Musaeus felt himself compelled to publish his *Vindiciae Disquisitionis;* which however only excited Grosse to a *Quarta defensio Triados.*

About the same time, the controversy was briskly carried on in Holland. D. Heinsius in his *Aristarchus Sacer,* and his *Exercitt. sac. in Nov. Testamentum,* had espoused the cause of Hellenism, and commented upon Pforscher's Diatribe. In a plainer manner still did he do this, in his *Exercitatio de Lingua Hellenistica,* published in 1643. In the very same year, the celebrated Salmasius appeared as his antagonist, in three separate publications, the spirit and tone of which may be readily discerned from their titles. The first was inscribed *Commentarius controversiam de lingua Hellenistica decidens;* the second, *Funus linguae Hellenisticae;* the third, *Ossilegium linguae Hellenisticae.*

In 1648, Gataker, in England, warmly espoused the cause of the Hellenists, in his *Dissert. de stilo Nov. Testamenti.* On the same side, about this time, appeared Werenfels of Switzerland, in his essay *De stylo script. Nov. Testamenti;* and J. Olearius, of Germany, in his book *De stylo Nov. Testamenti;* also Böckler, in his tract, *De ling.*

Nov. Test. originali. In Holland, Vorstius published, in defence of the same side, his book *De Hebraismis Nov. Testamenti*, 1658; and in 1665, his *Comment. de Hebraismis N. Test.* The last was attacked by H. Vitringa, in his *Specimen annotatt. ad philol. sac. Vorstii.*

The best of these Dissertations were collected and published by Rhenferd, in his *Syntagma Diss. philol. theol. de stilo Nov. Test,* 1703; and also by Van Honert, about the same time, at Amsterdam.

J. H. Michaelis, in his Essay *De textu Nov. Test,* Halae, 1707, and H. Blackwall in his *Sacred Classics illustrated and defended,* endeavoured to moderate the parties, and to show, that while it might safely be admitted that there are Hebraisms in the New Testament, it may at the same time be maintained, that the Greek of the sacred writers is entitled to the character of classic purity.

But all efforts at peace were defeated by Georgi of Wittemberg, who, in 1732, published his *Vindiciae Nov. Test.* This was answered by Knapp and Dressing of Leipsic. In 1733, Georgi published his *Hierocriticus Sacer,* in three books; and at the end of the year, a second part, in as many more books; which were also answered by his Leipsic opponents.

From this time, the cause of the Hellenists began to predominate throughout Europe. And though many essays on this subject have since appeared, and it has been canvassed in a far more able manner than before, yet few of these essays have been controversial; almost all writers leaning to the side of Hellenism.

Those who wish to satisfy their minds, on the point in question, may read *Campbell's Dissertations* perfixed to his *Translation of the Gospels;* or Ernesti's Chapter on this subject, in his *Institutio Interpretis.*

I should not have been thus prolix, on a topic which may seem somewhat foreign to my purpose, had I not an important end in view. Time has been, for a great number of years, when a man was regarded as a heretic by the majority of Protestants, because he believed that the New Testament writers did not compose in pure Attic Greek. It has now come to a state of things so widely different, that a man is universally regarded as an *ignoramus,* who does believe this. This may serve as a caution to those, who are disposed to make mere questions of criticism the *articuli stantis vel cadentis ecclesiae,* as if they entered into the essence of Christian belief. It may serve another purpose, viz, to remind all who are unacquainted with these subjects, that it is not safe to pronounce sentence upon them with confidence, and consign over to the infamy of unbelief, such as may differ from them in opinion with regard to such matters.   It may serve also to show, that men of exalted talents and knowledge, may sometimes contend in defence of points, which after all are either very unimportant ; or if important, must, to avoid serious evil to the church, be decided in opposition to their opinion.

To illustrate this, I would merely observe, that had the Attic character of the New Testament Greek been established, all internal evidence of the genuineness of the New Testament, drawn from its colouring and style, and serving to show that the men who wrote it were Hebrews, and that it is a *genuine* work, would fail.   As it is now, this evidence amounts to demonstration, in the mind of an unprejudiced critic.   What good then could all the zeal of Pforscher, Salmasius, Georgi, Pfochenius, and others effect?   Had they succeeded in their endeavours, they would have undermined one of the best internal evidences of the genuineness of the New Testament.

Men who contend, ought to learn what they are contending about, and what would be the result of their efforts, should they prove to be victorious.   If such were made indispensable conditions of enlisting under the banners of contention, there might be fewer combatants, less of hard names, and more of argument.   Above all, let men refrain from peremptory and absolute decision on mere questions of criticism, who have no means of understanding the state, the real object, or the final result of the points in question.   To condemn or to applaud is, in fact, equally unsafe, when we can give a good reason for neither the one nor the other.

Note G. page 20.

In regard to the view which Jahn has taken, of the aid which the kindred languages can afford to the biblical student, I apprehend there are some things omitted which are important, and some things represented in rather too strong colours.   He has set the Rabbinical commentators in their proper place, perhaps, if you regard them in many respects as expounders of the *sentiments* which the Old Testament contains.   But as mere Hebrew philologists, the Kimchi's Jarchi, Ben Gerson, Ben Melekh, Aben Ezra, and others deserve not so low a place.

It is true, that there are not, as Jahn says, any living or modern witnesses to the *usus loquendi* of the ancient Hebrews. But are there any of the Greek and Latin? Should you reply, We have modern Greek, and modern Latin; in my turn, I would answer, We have modern Hebrew too, in abundance; which holds just about the same relation to the ancient, as modern Latin and Greek to the ancient Roman and Attic. I admit that we have but very scanty remains of the ancient Hebrew tongue; but in the volume which we have, are comprised a great variety of authors, and all the varieties of composition. It is from a comparison of these, that the *usus loquendi* of the Hebrews is acquired; just as in reading Herodotus, and Homer, and Xenophon, we obtain the *usus loquendi* of the old Grecians and Attic writers. Can we not attain to this without a comparison of other languages, which may have an affinity with the Greek? I do not ask whether a knowledge of other languages may not cast some light on the subject of Greek idiom; but whether a man may not understand this idiom well, without a knowledge of them; and this, from reading and comparing the Greek writers themselves?

The answer I need not repeat. And a similar answer would I give, in regard to the Hebrew. The language itself furnishes the means, in regard to the great body of idiomatic expressions, of an explanation more or less satisfactory. But it needs thorough study, and nice, attentive observation to elicit it; and in what other language is not the case similar? In one respect too, the Hebrew has greatly the advantage of any dead language. There are complete Concordances of all the words in the language, by which the *usus loquendi* may be traced in every instance, in which any word occurs. This is not the case in respect to any other language.

Nor is it correct, to say that there are no good witnesses to the *usus loquendi* of the ancient Hebrew, except the kindred dialects. The Hellenistic Greek, in the Septuagint, in the Apocrypha, and in the New Testament, written by Jews who either spoke the Hebrew itself or a mixture of it with the Syriac or Chaldee which so nearly resemble it, is, *in a great multitude of instances*, a good witness to the point in question. The words indeed are Greek; but the language, i. e. the method of expression, the coloring, and the sense of the words are all conformed to the Hebrew mode of expression and thinking.

But having said thus much, to express my reasons for thinking Jahn's view of this topic a little too highly coloured; in justice to

him and to the subject, I must also express my views of the good
which the student is to expect, from the study of the kindred dialects
of the Hebrew.

In all the features which constitute the prominent traits of a language, the Syriac, Chaldee, Arabic, and Hebrew are the same.
Verbs of triliteral roots are the great basis of each. In respect to the
derivation of nouns, adjectives, and particles from these, and in regard to the forms of the derivates, there is a great similarity. The
inflections of the verb, (the ground form of the Shemitish languages,)
are nearly the same in all. The great rules of syntax, the mode of
forming sentences, the anomalies, the figures of speech, the peculiarities of expression, of imagery, the coloring derived from climate, man-
ners, dress, employments, &c, are all either the same, or very similar.
The words, in a multitude of cases, have the same significations in
each dialect.

Let the reader now ask, whether a person, specially a foreigner,
would be better able to acquire a thorough knowledge of the English
language, if he had acquired a good knowledge of the Norman,
French, Saxon, Latin, and Greek? Much more then, can one be
helped in his views of the Hebrew language, by a knowledge of the
cognate dialects ; which far more resemble the Hebrew, than the languages just mentioned do the English. In all the cognate dialects,
there are three classes of words which may be compared with the
Hebrew. First, a numerous class, where the meaning is the same in
each, or the variation from this very inconsiderable. In general,
words of this class are well understood by the study of the Hebrew
itself. But still, it is a great satisfaction to find confirmation of the
Hebrew sense, in the usage of the kindred languages. I have no
more doubt from reading the Hebrew alone, that מֶלֶךְ means *a king*,
than I have in regard to what *king* means in English. But when I
find the same word employed in the same sense, in Chaldee, Syriac,
and Arabic, the confirmation which this gives to the sense assigned, is
a very grateful thing to the mind, and leads it to feel, that the meaning of a multitude of Hebrew words can be confirmed with better evidence, than the meaning of an equal number in any other dead language whatever. For, as Jahn has finely said, " The Hebrew, though
dead, has living sisters of whom we may inquire respecting its appearance and character."

The second class of words are those, in which the coincidence of

11

meaning is but partial; there being several senses in one dialect, which are not attached to the same word in the other.

Here, it needs great caution and judgment to draw the lines of distinction, and fix the limits of each. And here, more mistakes have been made in applying the dialects to illustrate the Hebrew, than any where else. Suppose now that a Hebrew and Arabic word agree in three senses, and differ in three, each of which is well established by the common usage of each tongue; but in the Hebrew you meet the word in question, in a passage where the meaning appears dubious. On comparing the Arabic, you find that one of the senses, in which the word there commonly differs from the Hebrew, fits the passage well in Hebrew, and makes a meaning congruous, and well adapted to express the apparent sentiment of the author. In such a case, you might justly incline to admit the analogy of meaning between the Hebrew and Arabic word to extend somewhat farther than common usage would require; i. e. you may confirm an uncommon sense of the word in Hebrew, by a common one in Arabic.

I need scarcely add, that the light which may be thrown on many difficult passages in the Old Testament from such a source, must be of real, and oftentimes of *great* importance to the interpreter.

In regard to the third class of words, which do not appear to have any analogy of meaning as used in the Hebrew, and in the cognate dialects; great caution is needed in admitting them to control the sense of the Hebrew, in any case. It cannot indeed be affirmed, that because words of this sort do not *commonly* coincide in respect to sense, in the different dialects, that they *never* do so. But all which results from the application of such words to illustrate the Hebrew, amounts only to ·*probability*, never to *certainty*.

Thus far in regard to lexicography, or ascertaining the *sense* of words by comparison of the kindred languages, of which so extravagant a use has been made by Schultens, Michaelis, and many of their followers. In a multitude of cases, where the common Hebrew meaning of a word better fitted the passage, than any one drawn from the kindred languages, they have foisted in one from Arabic or Syriac, specially from the former. The Notes of Schultens upon Job, distinguished as they are for acquaintance with oriental learning, are deformed with this perpetual Arabic etymology. Reiske's *Conjecturae in Jobum*, the most extravagant work of this kind that has appeared, has long since ceased to excite any attention. Michaelis' *Supplementa ad Lex. Heb*, and Paulus' *Clavis* for Isaiah and the Psalms, furnish pretty complete specimens of what the Arabic *mania* can do, when unfettered with the sober rules of judicious philology.

The abuse of a good thing, however, is no argument against the use of it. But it shows the importance of rules to regulate that use. These have at last been prescibed by more sober philologists, such as Rosenmüller and Gesenius. The first in his Commentary, and the last in his Lexicon and Grammar, have shown us the true use of the kindred languages in illustrating the Hebrew. The sum of these rules is, that the kindred dialects have a more important bearing upon the *forms* and *syntax* of the Hebrew, than upon the meaning of its words, although the latter is by no means excluded. It is impossible for any one who does not study Gesenius, to see the exquisite use which he has made of the cognate dialects, to scatter light over obscure Hebrew *forms* and apparent *anomalies*. By what he has already done, he has shown how much may be done to illustrate the Hebrew, in such a use of the kindred languages.

The greatest work, which has yet appeared to aid the learner in a knowledge of the Arabic dialect, (the most important and difficult of all the cognate Shemitish dialects,) is the Arabic Grammar, pulished by Sylvestre De Sacy, at Paris, in A. D. 1810, in two volumes octavo. The history of this work is rather singular. The Directory of the French Republic, in the year 3 of the Republic, instituted a school of the living oriental languages at Paris, where their diplomatic agents, and some principal military officers were to be taught Arabic, Persian, Turkish, and some other languages, with a view to gain influence in the East, and to prepare the way for dispossessing the English of their eastern territory. In this school were placed several men of great abilities; and natives of different countries in the East were connected with it. The object of the Directory has been defeated; but the school remains : and not to mention others, the names of De Sacy, and Kieffer, and Coray* only are enough to give it celebrity, in Europe. There, are taught the Arabic, Turkish, Persian, Sanscrit, Armenian, and some other languages ; and there, in obedience to a law of the school, De Sacy, in 1810, published his Arabic Grammar ; an immortal work which consigns to obscurity, by its superior lustre, all previous works of the same nature ; and which has thrown more light upon the *forms* of words, the *idiom*,

---

* Now deceased.

and the *syntax* of the Shemitish languages, than has been cast before, for many centuries. By this work, which contains 462 pages of syntax, Gesenius has been substantially aided in the compilation of his Hebrew Grammar; and a multitude of things pertaining to the grammar and idiom of the Hebrew, (though they may be learned by the diligent student, without the aid of this work, so as to be useful to him,) are seen, without a knowledge of De Sacy's Arabic syntax, only as through a glass darkly. De Sacy has placed them in the meridian sun.

That a work, which was not designed to have the most remote bearing upon the Hebrew Scriptures, should be thus made to contribute in a signal manner to their illustration, ought surely to be a matter of gratitude to the great Disposer of events, who can overrule the designs of men to accomplish his own purposes.

The student can now find ample and excellent helps to the study of Chaldee, Syriac, and Arabic. Within a few years, all of these have been greatly multiplied in Germany. And after getting well master of the Hebrew forms and inflections, and proceeding so far as to read Hebrew with pleasure, he may, in a very short time, read the Chaldee Targums, or the Syriac New Testament. The Arabic is a more serious task. But enough of this, to reap the profit which he needs from its fundamental rules of syntax and idiom, he can acquire in a moderate space of time.

If the lovers of philology knew what treasures are locked up in the Arabic language, pure literary ardour, if no other motive operated, would be sufficient to induce them to cultivate this language. We call the Arabians barbarous, and regard them as a ferocious, uncultivated people. And it is certainly true, that in very ancient times they bore such a character, and that it may be applied to them, at present, in a greater 'or less degree. But it has not always been thus. While the dark ages of the Christian era were advancing, literature took its flight to Arabia, and sojourned in the capitals of the Caliphs, who wielded the destinies of the Mohammedam empire.* Many of these Caliphs were munificent patrons of literature. Who that is acquainted with the history of science, does not know that most of the modern sciences had their remote origin in Arabia? And it

---

* "Whilst all the nations of Europe were covered with the deepest shade of ignorance, the Caliphs in Asia encouraged the Mohammedans to improve their talents, and cultivate the fine arts; and even the Turkish Sultan, who drove the Greeks from Constantinople, was a patron of literary merit, and was himself an elegant poet." (Pref. to Persian Grammar, by Sir William Jones, p. VI.)

needs nothing but an acquaintance with the writers which Arabia has produced, to know that this country has been very prolific in writers of every kind, whether scientific, historic, poetic, or philological.

Finer specimens of narration than De Sacy has presented in his Arabic Chrestomathy, cannot well be found, I believe, in Herodotus, Thucydides, or Xenophon. Some of the Arabic poetry too may well vie with any thing of a similar kind, contained in either Greek or Latin authors. In the science of grammar and lexicography, before literature began to revive in Europe, the Arabians had gone beyond what we have yet reached ; at any rate, what we have reached in the English language. The Grammar of De Sacy is taken principally from the Arabic grammarians. The great lexicon of Golius is compiled principally from Jauhari, with occasional comparison of other Arabic lexicographers ; and is executed in such a manner as to make one blush for even such a work as Johnson's Dictionary. Not only has it quoted authorities to justify the sense of words as Johnson has, but all the verbs are exhibited in compound as well as simple construction, (i. e. as followed by prepositions, adverbs, &c, of all sorts,) and all the shades of meaning and syntax in this compound construction are given. And in regard to Grammar, if De Sacy presents a fair specimen of the Arabian knowledge of this subject, (as no doubt he does,) our best works of this nature may well retreat from comparison with those of Arabia.

These attainments, let it be remembered, were made, when gross darkness covered the Christian world ;* and with all our improvements in the knowledge of grammar and lexicography, many years will yet pass, before we shall reach the summit which Arabia attained almost a thousand years ago, in these sciences.

Does the philologist need still further excitement to search for the hidden treasures of this peculiar nation, he may find it in the nature of the language itself. The copiousness and flexibility of the Greek language has been the standing theme of exultation among Greek critics, for centuries past ; and with good reason. But had these critics better known the Arabic, some of their encomiums might have been pronounced on this. Like the Greek, the Arabic has a dual of verbs, nouns, adjectives, participles, and pronouns. It has three

* Jauhari, whose work forms the basis of Golius' Lexicon, flourished in the eleventh Century, (the midnight of European darkness;) and Fitsurabadi whose work is the basis of Giggeus' Arabic Lexicon in 4 vols. folio, flourished in the thirteenth Century.

cases in each number. The verb has four forms of the future tense ; and instead of a mere active, passive, and middle voice, it has twenty four conjugations, thirteen active and eleven passive, with futures, imperatives, infinitives, and participles : one half of which conjugations convey shades and colours of meaning that no Greek conjugation or voice can designate, and which the Greek language, in a multitude of cases, can scarcely even by periphrasis express. As to the derivatives from verbs—all the conjugations, active and passive, have participles, with three forms in the singular, as many in the dual, and also in the plural ; which may be used, as verbs, adjectives, nouns, or adverbs. In addition to this, the infinitive mood of the first conjugation only has not less than thirty-three forms, which may be used as verbs, nouns, or adverbs. From these, nouns are formed with an almost endless variety of phases. Beside the regular plural, there is a plural, (more commonly used than the regular one,) called the *plural-is fractus* from its irregularity, which is made by an internal mutation of words instead of change at the end. Of this, thirty species at least may be formed of almost any single noun ; and the variety which actually exists is far greater than this, and, with all the phases that are occasioned by the quiescent letters, amounts to several hundred forms. To augment this endless variety, there are intensive nouns, adjectives, participles, verbs (made by conjugation,) and adverbs, of many forms and declensions.

The delicacy of shade in many Arabic forms, is beyond any thing of which I have any knowledge, in any other language. A verb, for instance, may signify to *do a thing*, to *cause another to do it*, to *do it in company with another*, to *do it in contention with another or in opposition to him*, to *do it intensely*, to *feign to do it*, to *do it habitually or repeatedly*, to *ask that it should be done*, to *regard it as done*, to *do it upon one's self*, to *do it for one's self*, &c. All this and much more is expressed simply by *conjugation*, which, applied to the Arabic, means a different mode of inflecting the same verb ; and all these conjugations have a passive as well as an active voice ; and a masculine and feminine gender.

In regard to nouns—the shades of some of the forms are exquisite. One form denotes an action performed *only a single time ;* another variation of the same word denotes *habitual action* of the same kind ; one form of the plural denotes a few ; another a great multitude. Some forms of nouns mark an action done with zeal, and energy ; others with remissness. To agree with nouns of every sort, verbs, participles and adjectives have a masculine and feminine form, and a singular, dual, and plural number.

Let now the admirers of the Greek copiousness and inflection contemplate this picture, which is but a very faint and imperfect likeness, and then say, if the Greek is worth cultivating for its copiousness and variety, whether the Arabic is not entitled to a much higher degree of attention still, so far as these qualities are concerned.

As to variety of inflection, the above representation may give some idea of it. As to copiousness, one fact more may be mentioned. Golius' lexicon of the Arabic is a folio, closely printed in double columns, and containing nothing but mere explanations and constructions, and yet containing about three thousand columns. The common allegation that the Arabic has five hundred names for the lion, though not strictly correct, yet may serve to give an impressive idea of the copiousness of the language.

Nothing can account for the *universal neglect* of this language (which is perhaps the most perfect and the most extensively spoken of any language on earth,) among our countrymen, but the want of knowledge in respect to the treasures which it contains.

To complete this protracted note ; may it not be well concluded then, that no student should neglect to cultivate the kindred languages, who can be master of time, resolution, and expense enough to acquire a knowledge of them ? But alas ! where must he go, for a master to direct his studies ? Not a school in all America, where the very rudiments of these languages are taught, by any provision made for this purpose ! How long is money to be hoarded up, or lavished upon worthless objects, or sacrificed to defend an imaginary and chivalrous point of honour, while knowledge which would cast great light upon the word of God, and heighten the reputation of our country, may seek in vain for a solitary patron, in this land of liberty and of illumination ? It would confer a lasting honour on the nation, or on any state, or private individual, to institute a school of such a nature, that the oriental languages, in all their branches, and with an ample apparatus, might be pursued, by those who aim at a distinguished knowledge, either of literature or of the Scriptures. It is an object too, in which all denominations of Christians might unite. May some enlightened patrons speedily arise, to imitate in this interesting department of literature what has been recently done by distinguished benefactors, dead and living, in various departments of theology and science !

NOTE H. page 22.

What Jahn has here said, by way of comparing the former and the present state of science in Germany, will apply in many respects to our own country. Science of almost every kind is making advances here. In regard to theology; such is the unhappy division of opinion on some of its fundamental topics, that it has become quite necessary for those who mean to choose and maintain their ground, to become well versed in Biblical interpretation. A contest of no trifling nature is begun; and it is not to be expected that it will cease, during the present generation. The times call for a well grounded knowledge of the Bible among theologians, above any other acquisition except ardent piety.

Many of our Clergy, of the last and the preceding generation, were men of powerful minds and elevated piety. They have left not a few monuments behind them, of forcible argument and sound reasoning in theology. But might they not have risen higher still, had they been able interpreters of the Scriptures? And shall we sit down contented with what they acquired, without striving to add something to the common stock, which is to benefit the church? The enlightened youth, who aims at distinguished usefulness as the dictate of Christian benevolence, will not be at a loss to answer this question.

NOTE I. page 23.

The truth of these remarks, I do most fully believe, can be made out by appeal to experience. If a man really loves study—has an eager attachment to the acquisition of knowledge—nothing but peculiar sickness or misfortunes will prevent his being a student, and his possessing in some good degree the means of study. The fact is that when men complain of want of time for study, and want of means, they only show that, after all, they are either attached to some other objects of pursuit, or have no part or lot in the spirit of a student. They will applaud others, it may be, who do study, and look with some degree of satisfaction, or a kind of wonder upon their acquisitions; but for themselves, they cannot spare the time nor expense necessary to make such acquisitions; or they put it to the account of their humility, and bless themselves that they are not *ambitious*. In most of all these cases, however, either the love of the world, or genuine laziness, lies at the bottom. Had they more energy and decision of character, and did they redeem the precious moments which they now lose in laboriously doing nothing, or nothing to the purpose of the church, they might open all the treasures of the East and the West, and have them at their disposal. I might safely promise good knowledge of Hebrew and Greek to most men of this sort, if they would diligently improve the time that they now absolutely throw away, in the course of three or four years. While one man is deliberating whether he had better study a language, another man has obtained it. Such is the difference between decisive, energetic action, and a timid, hesitating, indolent manner of pursuing literary acquisitions. And what is worst of all in this temporizing class of students, is, that if you reason with them and convince them that they are pursuing a wrong course, that conviction operates no longer than until the next paroxysm of indolence, or of a worldly spirit comes on. These Syren charmers lull every energetic power of the mind to sleep. The mistaken man, who listens to their voice, finds himself at the age of forty, just where he was at thirty. At fifty, his decline has already begun. At sixty, he is universally regarded with indifference; which he usually repays with misanthropy. And if he has the misfortune to live until he is seventy, every body is uneasy because he is not transferred to a better world.

Set such a picture before the indolent student, and he will probably say, It is caricature. But if he be candid enough to admit the correctness of the portrait, and to have some temporary pangs of conviction that he is pursuing a wrong course—if the malady be driven away for a short time, he will relapse. *Si naturam furcâ expellas, usque recurret.*

But to be more serious ; the God who has given to men talents and opportunities both for intellectual and moral culture, demands of all men that they should cultivate them in such a manner, as to attain the highest point of usefulness in their power. The servant who " was afraid, and went and hid his master's talent in the earth," was met with an awful frown by his Lord. How can any servant in the ministry account to his Lord, for having failed to reach one half the extent of usefulness in his power, through want of mental exertion ? Let those make light of it, who will ; the Captain of our Salvation does not expect his soldiers to sleep upon their posts, nor to neglect the discipline or duties which he enjoins.

12

NOTE K. page 24.

This paragraph contains a very just statement, of the manner in which Biblical learning should be used by those who possess it. The same sentiment may be expressed in a manner somewhat different. "The interpreter should not exhibit the *process* of exegesis in his public discourses, but the *results* of it." This very simple and intelligible rule, if adhered to, will save a man from the appearance of being pedantic in the pulpit ; while it communicates to his hearers the benefit of all his private studies. Nothing can be more disgusting, than to hear a preacher, before a common audience, interlard his discourse with Latin, Greek, and Hebrew quotations. Nor is this in any degree necessary, in order that an audience should profit by the philological labours of the preacher. The simple rule above laid down will guide him safely, in respect to this point of his duty.

----●●●----

NOTE L. page 29.

Religious controversy is in itself an evil, and to be deprecated, inasmuch as it not unfrequently excites animosity, and parties contend for victory, not for truth. But, like most other evils in the world, it is very often overruled by the great Head of the Church, to accomplish very important purposes. Controversy elicits mental effort ; and makes extensive investigation necessary. Many of the greatest efforts of the human mind, which have elucidated and established truths of the highest moment, have been occasioned by controversy. Besides, opponents to a good cause serve to discover any flaws in the building which has been erected. The building reared by the Reformation has been powerfully assailed, first by Catholics, and then of late by a multitude of keen-sighted critics, who reject the idea of any thing supernatural, either in regard to the composition of the Bible itself, or in respect to the facts which it relates. The result has been, that while the building still stands, many a piece of timber, which was once framed into it, and regarded as important to its strength, or its symmetry, has been thrown away as useless, or condemned as unsound. More still are doubtless to be laid aside. But the basis, the corner posts, the pillars, and all the *essential* parts of the frame, still remain. The storms which have beat upon them, have only compacted them more firmly together. My heart exults in the belief, that if the floods come and the winds blow, they will continue to stand. I must believe that their foundation is the Rock of Ages; and that they were framed together by that hand, which stretched out the heavens, and which moves suns and stars in their harmonious order.

There is one point of view, then, in which the Christian can rejoice, even in the opposition that is made to that cause, which he regards as most sacred and important. The truth, by opposition and consequent discussion, will be made to relinquish all its insufficient, unstable supports, and rely only on those which will stand the test of ages. On this *result*, I can look with most sincere satisfaction ; although Christian benevolence might lead me to weep over the means, by which the truths of the gospel are to be subjected to their fiery trial. The sheet anchor of the pious soul, in the midst of all the storms that arise, is, *The Lord reigns;* and *All things shall work together for good to those who love God.*

I cannot conlude this note, without protesting, with Jahn, against charging all the theological controversies that rise up, upon philological studies. The real truth is, that if men had a right temper of mind, the study of Hermeneutics would remove most if not all of their differences of opinion about the doctrines of the Scriptures. The science of Hermeneutics prescribes rules for interpreting the Scriptures, founded in the common sense and reason of all men, and independent of all party and local views ; and just so far as they produce their proper influence, they bring men to unite in their views of the meaning of Scripture. In fact, I know of no means so powerful, or at least which promises so much, in regard to removing the difference of opinion among Christians, as such a common law, which is independent of all parties and a tribunal to which all must appeal, unless it be the spirit of benevolence and kindness. This indeed holds the first rank among all the graces which adorn the kingdom of the Redeemer. It is then for the want of this—it is from prejudice, from ignorance, from local, party, selfish views, that men abuse criticism, and make it the means of defending heresies, and lighting the flame of controversy. Have they not acted in the same manner, when scholastic, or metaphysical theologizing was the order of the day ? And will they not always pervert every good gift, when led away by passion and prejudice, until their hearts are cured of the raging malady which inflames them ?

In short, is the *abuse* of a thing any solid objection against its importance and usefulness? If so, then the Creator has erred in shedding the light of day over our benighted world, because so many abuse it to purposes of malevolence; and Christianity itself—that diviner light, which beams from the throne of God upon our race wandering in death-shade, is to be regarded only as darkness.

NOTE M. page 48.

It will be easily seen, from comparing the remarks which Jahn, Michaelis, and Gesenius make upon the common mode of teaching languages at the German Universities, that it differs greatly from the method usually practised in this country. In the public or class lectures there, the teacher dictates every thing, at the commencement; and the student, unless he has a brazen memory, must write it down upon the spot, and con it over at his lodgings. He has no part to perform at these lectures, except to copy what is said. The lecturer is a grammar, and dictionary, and commentary, all at the same time. In private lectures, the student seeks and may obtain whatever privileges he needs, in respect to asking questions, translating, or performing any other scholastic exercise. He may employ his teacher as he wishes, during the hour which is devoted to him.

With this in view, the reader of the preceding dissertations will be able easily to understand all that is there said about lectures and private exercises.

In this country, we are as yet so little accustomed to strict method and discipline in pursuing our studies, that it would be hazardous to speak positively on the method of the German discipline. Thus much we may safely say. As we have no establishments of such a nature, that students can enjoy public and private instruction in the German method, so we cannot conform to that method, in all respects. May I not venture also to say, that no method of instruction can be very profitable to a young man, which does not call into strenuous exercise the *active* powers of the mind? He must LEARN TO THINK, and not become a mere receptacle for the thoughts of others.

In regard to the best method of teaching, Gesenius and Jahn agree, in all that is important. The plan of dictating *orally* to beginners, however, I cannot persuade myself is a happy way of teaching. From experience I can testify, that it is extremely tedious to the teacher, and enables the learner to make but a slow and uncertain progress. Much better is it, that his elementary books should be so composed, as to save the time and tedium of writing down all he learns, until he can begin to write understandingly. But a great fault is often committed, in the composition of such books. For the most part, they are either composed so as to make the student *passive* in his acquisitions; or else they are left in such a state, that the beginner is unable to make any satisfactory progress in them. The study of books, which hold a middle way between these, united with recitations in which the student must take an active part, and may have all his errors corrected and his difficulties solved, accompanied with so much of criticism and commentary (varied according to circumstances) as shall give him a relish for his author, disclose to him his beauties and his faults, and help him to form a correct and elevated taste, would seem to hold out as good a prospect of improvement, as any method which can be adopted.

In Hebrew, elementary books of the class above named are few and not easily to be procured. In Latin and Greek, they are very numerous. But many of them are very poorly adapted to beginners. For example, the *Selecta* in Latin, and the *Graeca Minora*, contain some as hard Latin and Greek as is to be found in the whole range of classic writers. Is this adapted to *learners?* I might ask— Is it adapted to teachers? Many of the latter class are unable to help their pupils out of the difficulties, which these selections present.

As to the last point mentioned above, viz, lecturing on the style, sentiments, beauties, and defects of classic authors, and intermixing explanations historical, geographical, literary, &c, I would ask, what is done of all this, in our schools and colleges? Here is a substantial defect in our mode of study, that calls loudly for redress. A boy may now read Virgil through, without obtaining a knowledge of any thing more than his Latin words, which he might almost as well have learned by studying his lexicon. In this way he is brought up to be a mere superficial reader of classics.* He knows not what treasures they contain, and of course, feeling little or no interest in them, he lays aside the study of them as soon as he can.

This is one of the grand points, which gives a European education in the classics so decided a preference over ours. When shall we learn, that youth need to be taught the *elements* of *taste* for reading, and to be led to a critical, hermeneutical, and rhetorical study of every author which they peruse? All our efforts at instruction, while

* Since this was first printed, some of our colleges have made arrangements which will lead, it is hoped, to a much better method of study.

this is neglected, are but little better than mechanical, and must fail
to produce the highest and best effect. This is most manifest from
the fact, that the great body of our young men, who study the classics
at schools and colleges, never imbibe taste enough for them to pursue
them in after life.

The spirit of these remarks may be applied, in its full force, to
the study of the original languages of the Scriptures. Of what worth
is a knowledge of Greek and Hebrew words, without any taste or talent for the exegesis of the Scriptures? The mere knowledge of
words is worthless; and unless the Scriptures are studied in such a
way as to acquire a definite knowledge of the ideas which the words
designate, the learner may as well be employed in studying Chero-
kee as Hebrew.

There is one other view of the subject in hand, which I cannot
forbear taking, before I conclude this miscellaneous note. I have
reference to such a method of study, as shall form and cultivate a
proper sense of the beauties of composition in the Scriptural writers.
Many serious persons seem to feel as if it were a kind of impiety, or at
least a glaring evidence of want of spiritual-mindedness, when any
one speaks of being charmed with the beauties of the Scriptures.
That there are those, who find no other beauties in them than some
fine figures and energetic expressions, I am very ready to concede.
That a man may read them, also, and be an ardent admirer of their
style, which exhibits so much simplicity, dignity, and moral sublimity, and yet have no practical regard at all either to the doctrines or
precepts which they inculcate, I grant with equal readiness. But
then I must be permitted to ask, Cannot the moral and mental faculties both be addressed, through the medium of the Scriptures? In
that other book of God, whose characters are engraven upon every
part of the earth on which we stand, and inscribed with beams of
suns and stars on the volume of the sky, are there no *beauties* display-
ed, and none which it is proper to perceive? For what purpose did he,
who spread his glory abroad over the heavens, and decked the earth
with countless beauties, form in man (created in his own image too)
a power to perceive, and a taste to relish such charms as these?
Was it to be gratified, or suppressed? And when he has scattered, with
greater profusion still, diviner charms and glories over the pages of
Revelation, shall we do violence to our natures, and close our senses
against the perception or relish of them? Each one may answer
his question as he will—but for me, I would that I had a thousand

senses instead of the very limited number which I possess, provided
they might all be avenues to the divine beauties of the sacred pages!

The God of nature undoubtedly designed, that his glory as dis-
played in the works of his hands, should lead him who contemplates it
to its great author.   Unbelief and ingratitude may choose another path;
and while they enjoy the gift, may deny or contemn the giver.   But
the Christian makes a very different use of the enjoyments, which
the gratification of his taste for the beauties of nature procures for
him.   And so it is, in respect to the Scriptures.   One man may relish the beauty of composition, but neglect the proper use of it.   Another is excited by the same to a higher relish, to more intense study,
and to a more exalted admiration of the word of God.   If I have a
pious heart, why can I not improve in the cultivation of a Christian
spirit by reading the Scriptures, while at the same time my taste is
gratified, and my curiosity excited to the highest degree?

If this view is just, then a mere study of the *words* of Scripture,
without entering into all the spirit, meaning, and beauty of the
sacred writers, is a very defective, dry, unpromising method of study.
Those who feel as if they ought to see nothing but the traces of the
original curse upon the face of the earth, and would fain look upon
the glories of the sky, as veiled in everlasting eclipse—may turn
aside from cultivating a relish for the beauties of the Bible, with
some degree of consistency.   But the Christian, who exults in the reflection of divine radiance from the earth and sky, and in the brighter image of it in the Scriptures of truth, will thank God that he has giv-
en him understanding to perceive, and a heart to relish such beauties.

May I venture one step further, and ask, Is not the dry and fruit-
less manner in which the Scriptures are read in most cases, one reason why so few, who are not Christians, have a relish for them?   Is
it true, that Homer, and Virgil, and other heathen writers have so far
surpassed, in the beauties of composition, the holy authors of the
Bible?   I answer; No.   If one half as much pains were taken in
the critical study of the Bible, as is bestowed on heathen writers, the
relish for it would be higher, even as a matter of taste, than for them.
Why then will not the mere man of taste study the Scriptures, in
order to gratify that taste?   The only reason is, that the common
mode of studying them is so dry and forbidding to him, that he cannot be allured by it.

Are we then, I shall be asked, to recommend the study of the
Scriptures as a matter of scholarship and taste?   Undoubtedly not,

simply as a matter of taste ?   Not because the Scriptures have not a
high claim to be thus studied, even supposing they stood upon the
same basis with heathen writings ; but because we believe them to
be designed not only for this, but for a much more exalted and noble
object.   Would any object to requesting an unbeliever to attend wor-
ship, at a particular church, because the minister was a man of a fine
cultivated taste, and commanding eloquence ?   And might not even
this be held out as an inducement, to persuade the unbeliever to go
where he could hear the truth ?

If so, then I may recommend the study of the Scriptures, for many reasons ; and one of these may be, that they present some of the
finest specimens of beauty and sublimity to be found in any writings
that exist.   Who knows, but that while the reader is charmed with
their pages, he may become humble, and broken-hearted, under the
influence of their instruction ?*

To conclude ; whether we study the classics or the Scriptures,
no reasonable person will contend, that we ought not to aim at a full
perception and enjoyment of all their meaning and their beauties.
To stop at this as an ultimate end, would be mere literary Epicure-
anism.   But to use it as means of rousing us to exertion, is surely
as rational, as to set before men the rewards of virtue, in order to
allure them to the practice of it.

If the reader of this note is convinced that the principles which
it defends are correct—let him pause, and ask, if a thorough reformation in the *mode of teaching and studying the classics, sacred and pro-
fane,* has not become absolutely necessary, to do justice to the rising
generation of our country.

---

* In a discourse delivered by Sir William Jones, the president of the Ben-
gal Society for Asiatic Researches, &c, in 1791, this admirable scholar, who
had at his command all the treasures of the East and West, says, " Theological inquiries are no part of my present subject ; but I cannot refrain from ad-
ding, that the collection of Tracts, which we call from their excellence, *the
Scriptures,* contain, independently of a divine origin, *more true sublimity, more
exquisite beauty, purer morality, more important history, and finer strains both
of poetry and eloquence, than could be collected within the same compass, from
all other books that were ever composed in any age, or any idiom.*"
                    ASIAT. RESEARCH. ED. 5. VOL. III. p. 15.

www.ingramcontent.com/pod-product-compliance
Lightning Source LLC
Chambersburg PA
CBHW070515090426
42735CB00012B/2798